FROM PAST REVIEWS

In her descriptive pieces she exercises such admirable art in epithet and observation. These poems should appeal to a public that appreciates sensitive, poetic craftsmanship and lucid utterance.
SIEGFRIED SASSOON (1948)

She treads safely among great themes. Like Emily Bronte or an Eleanor Farjeon, she can unbearably convey the desolation of loss. Her nature poetry joins observation, precise as a naturalist's, to heart-catching metaphor and image.
Times Literary Supplement (1948)

Phoebe Hesketh writes with great strength and many critics have compared her with Emily Bronte. Her emotional power is balanced by her intellectual resources. She deals in ideas as well as feelings.
ROY CAMPBELL, *Poetry Review* (1954)

Phoebe Hesketh is one of England's strongest and most genuine poets. For chilling, uncompromising vision, courage and a distinctive feminine compassion, no woman has written a better book of poems in all the recent years of woman-consciousness.
ANNE STEVENSON, *Times Literary Supplement* (1977)

A poet of great purity and strength whose work, miraculously, continues to develop. She has been absurdly underrated.
A. ALVAREZ, *The Observer* (1978)

Phoebe Hesketh's new collection is a constant delight. Reading the book with a notebook on one knee, intending to scribble down the odd telling phrase or image, this reviewer found himself copying down whole poems and trying to learn them.
IAN McMILLAN, *Poetry Review* (1989)

'*Netting the Sun*' remains an intensely rewarding book distinguished by a lucid intelligence and a quiet dignity which should put many flashier poets to shame.
NEIL POWELL, *P.N. Review* (1989)

Hesketh is by no means the gentle lyrical miniaturist she might appear, and in her eighties has lost none of her flair for close observation.
ALAN BROWNJOHN, *The Sunday Times* (1992)

BY THE SAME AUTHOR

POETRY

Poems (Sherratt and Hughes, Manchester 1939)
Lean Forward Spring! (Sidgwick and Jackson, London, 1948)
No Time for Cowards (Heinemann, London, 1952)
Out of the Dark (Heinemann, London, 1954)
Between Wheels and Stars (Heinemann, London, 1956)
The Buttercup Children (Hart-Davis, London, 1958)
Prayer for the Sun (Hart-Davis, London, 1966)
A Song of Sunlight (Chatto and Windus, London, 1974)
Preparing to Leave (Enitharmon, London, 1977)
The Eighth Day (Enitharmon, London, 1980)
A Ring of Leaves (Hayloft Press, Birmingham, 1985)
Over the Brook (Taxus, Leicester, 1986)
Netting the Sun: New and Collected Poems (Enitharmon, Petersfield 1989)
Sundowner (Enitharmon, London 1992)
The Leave Train: New and Collected Poems (Enitharmon, London 1994)
A Box of Silver Birch (Enitharmon, London 1997)

PROSE

My Aunt Edith (Peter Davies, London, 1966)
Second Edition (Lancashire County Books, 1992)
Rivington: The story of a village (Peter Davies, London, 1972)
Second Edition (Country Book Club, Newton Abbott, 1974)
What Can the Matter Be? (United Writers, Penzance, 1985)
Rivington: Village of the Mountain Ash (Carnegie, Preston, 1990)

PHOEBE HESKETH

THREADS OF SONG

*Collected Poems
1925–2001*

COMMEMORATIVE COLLECTION

AUSTIN MACAULEY PUBLISHERS™
LONDON • CAMBRIDGE • NEW YORK • SHARJAH

Copyright © The Estate of Phoebe Hesketh (2021)

The right of Phoebe Hesketh to be identified as author of this work has been asserted in accordance with section 77 and 78 of the Copyright, Designs and Patents Act 1988.

All rights reserved. No part of this publication may be reproduced, stored in a retrieval system, or transmitted in any form or by any means, electronic, mechanical, photocopying, recording, or otherwise, without the prior permission of the publishers.

Any person who commits any unauthorized act in relation to this publication may be liable to criminal prosecution and civil claims for damages.

A CIP catalogue record for this title is available from the British Library.

ISBN 9781528999069 (Paperback)
ISBN 9781528999076 (ePub e-book)

www.austinmacauley.com

First Published (2021)
Austin Macauley Publishers Ltd
25 Canada Square
Canary Wharf
London
E14 5LQ

PREFACE

Phoebe Hesketh was the eldest daughter of the pioneer radiologist A.E. Rayner and his wife, Gertrude who was an accomplished violinist. She was born in Preston in 1909. The previously unpublished poem 'Return to Ribblesdale Place' (p. 182) is a wistful recollection of her birthplace. She was educated at Cheltenham Ladies College. She married in 1931, had three children, and for many years lived with her family in the small Lancashire village she wrote about in her prose books *Rivington* (1972) and *Village of the Mountain Ash* (1990). She died in 2005.

At a junior school for girls in Southport, she discovered she had a knack for writing poetry. Thanks to her English teacher, words became a fascination, leaping into scansion and rhyme. For her they were evocative and, when imaginatively related to each other, assumed a quality akin to that of magic: making poetry out of prose. This fascination continued throughout her career, as is clear in 'Words' (p. 106).

Her Petrarchan sonnet, the first poem in Part Two, 'Poems for Younger Readers', won the Cheltenham Ladies' College poetry prize in 1925.

She left school soon afterwards to nurse her sick mother. After her mother's death in 1928, and for the next twenty-three years she wrote little poetry, apart from her first volume *Poems*, published in 1939 and dismissed later as 'juvenile'.

Nevertheless, her delightful rhythmic poem 'Who and Why' is included in Part 2 of this collection (p. 161).

Before her marriage, she walked frequently in the north Lancashire countryside and moorland with which she identified herself with much feeling. Her poem 'Northern Stone' (p. 25) declares 'All these are my lifestream, scoured and thinned.'

During the Second World War she was appointed part-time editor of the *Bolton Evening News* Women's page. Her brief was to write 'simple, clear prose – no fine writing – which has something to say and says it in words well chosen, apt and pared to the minimum'. These instructions later underpinned the flair, fluency and concise nature of her poetry.

Her career as a poet began in 1945 with her collaboration with the poet Herbert Palmer. His insistence on uncomplicated diction led to the simplicity and directness of her lyric poetry, making it all the more potent and surprising.

Lean Forward Spring, published in 1948, was followed by nine volumes and three collections before the publication of her last volume *A Box of Silver Birch* in 1997.

She was awarded the Greenwood prize for poetry in 1948 and 1967.

She followed no fashion, though her imagery and themes have a contemporary quality. Her poetry, a match between sound and sense, is original and lyrical. It is the outcome of restless, but intellectual argument and a determination to make words work without descending into irritable obscurities.

Her originality lay in her ability to use accepted forms and subject matter to shine new light on whatever she wanted to express.

She had little time for poetry that was written, as she would say, 'from the top of the head', rather than 'from the heart'. At the end of her career she wrote: 'I am that unfortunate thing, a lyric poet. Oh, hard to cut out the tongue of a natural bard and leave it all to the brain.'

In 1956 she was elected a Fellow of the Royal Society of Literature. In 1990, in recognition of her significant contribution to poetry, she was elected a Fellow of the University of Central Lancashire.

ACKNOWLEDGEMENTS

I would like to thank my wife Jutta, my family and friends, and Stephen Stuart-Smith who have supported me, given me advice and encouragement during the preparation of this commemorative collection of my mother's poems.

In addition, I would like to thank Chris Beamish for the secretarial services she provided during the preparation of this collection.

I would like to thank Walter Stephenson for his thorough and close reading of the poems and advising me of inconsistencies, which I have taken into account and remedied.

INTRODUCTION

The title of this commemorative collection of my mother's lyrical poetry was prompted by 'A Thread of Song', the title of the third section of her collection *Out of the Dark* published in 1954. The title is particularly felicitous, as my father was a Master Cotton Spinner. He is present in two poems of this collection: 'The Mill Clock' (p. 109) and 'Master Cotton Spinner' (p. 130).

In the preface to her volume *No Time for Cowards* Herbert Palmer wrote: 'Song comes readily to her because it is the natural expression of her spirit and uncomplicated passion.'

The aim of this collection of published and unpublished poems written in later life is to attract readers to her poetry which is not as widely appreciated as it should be.

This commemorative collection is in three parts: published poems, poems for younger readers and unpublished poems.

Part One reveals the 'threads of song' woven throughout her poems and the gradual evolution of her poetry beginning in her late thirties. Her first brisk, immediate poems with lilting cadences are seamlessly followed by poems that are more lyrical, reflective and succinct.

The poems in the second part are for younger readers, beginning with the 1925 prize-winning sonnet and followed by the poem 'Who and Why' referred to in the Preface.

The third part features late poems not published previously. They were discovered recently, amongst many others, during a review of papers after her death. They are included because they give a wider window into the poet and person she was.

Martin Hesketh

CONTENTS

PART ONE
PUBLISHED POEMS

From *Lean Forward Spring* (1948)
Tom Rich 16
Lyric Evening 18
St. Luke's Summer 19
The Tyrants 1942 20
Between the Thought and the Word 21
The Dipper 22
The Pedlar 23
Search 24

From *No Time for Cowards* (1952)
Northern Stone 25
Giraffes 26
Zebras 27
I Am Not Resigned 28
It Was Not I 29
Over the Water 30
Blue Tits 31
Nothing Grows Old 31
The Old Lead Mines 32
Drought 33
A Christmas Tree Speaks 34
The Open Door 35

From *Out of the Dark* (1954)
Wordsworth's Old Age 36
The Mallard 37
Prayer for Sun 38
She 38
Walking on Air 39
Breath of All the World 39
Snow 40
Midsummer 41
The Swifts 42
In Praise of Darkness 42

From *Between Wheels and Stars* (1956)
Integration 43
Skeleton Bride 44
Imagination 45
John Clare Dreaming 46
Spring in a City 47
Geraniums Are Verbs 48
I Have Not Seen God 49
A Poem in an Old Man's Heart 50
In Silverwell Street 51

From *The Buttercup Children* (1958)
The Buttercup Children 52
House in the Tree 53
The Fox 54
Bleasedale; the Wooden Circle 55
Reclaimed 57
Recapitulation 59
Love Without Frontiers 60
Evergreen 60
The Vine 61
Village Postman 62
Ploughing 63

From *Prayer for the Sun* (1966)
Harlequin 64
Heron 64
Fisherman Poet 65
Death of a Gardener 66
He Saved Others 67
Geriatric Ward 68
The Dark Side of the Moon 69
Dilemma 70
The Palomino 71
Seed Time 72

From *Preparing to Leave* (1977)
Beginning 73
Rise 74
And Fall 74
The Horses 75
I Give Death to a Son 76
Boy Drowning 77

Cross	78
Old Corinth	79
Museum	80
Brief Encounter	81
I Cannot Look into the Sun	82
Preparing to Leave	83
The Meths Men	84

From *The Eighth Day* (1980)

Journey	85
What Is God?	87
Letter to Vincent	88
Call of the North	89
Joie de Mourir	90
Stranger	91
Prisoners	92
Renaissance	92
In the Beginning	93
I Am	94
Refugees	95

From *Over the Brook* (1986)

Violet at Ninety	96
Yew Tree Guest House	97
Analyst	98
On Wansfell	98
Parting at a Country Station	99
Hobson's Choice	100
Waiting	101
A Very Small Casualty	102
Credo	103
After Ecclesiastes	104
Unicorn	105

From *Netting the Sun* (1989)

Words	106
Bolton-Le-Moors, 1960	107
The Betterware Man	108
The Mill Clock	109
Love's Advocate	110
Loneliness Is a Lyric Poem	111
Clown	112
Paint Box	113

Boy with Kite 114
Limbo 115
Understudy 116
Reply to a Philistine 116
A Child's Guide to Philosophy 117
Scapegoat 118
Emily Dickinson 118
The Party 119
Autumn at Whitewell 120
Roots 121
Sun Up 122

From *Sundowner* (1992)
Partridge 123
Orpheus in the Underground 124
Protean Lover 124
Starlings 125
The Shaping Spirit 126
No Reply at Christmas 127
Return 128
Vision 129
Edward Thomas 129
Master Cotton Spinner 130
Imprint 133
All Hallows 134
Sundowner 134
Being 135
Olympia 136
Perennial Love Song 137
Shutting Out the Sun 137
Prophet 138

From *The Leave Train* (1994)
A Poem Is a Painting 139
Naked Ostrich 140
Changing Colour 141
Comparison with a Sunflower 141
So Little It Can Take 142
After Verlaine 142
Walking Back 143
The Gymnasts 144
From Walden 145

Days 147
Defeathered 147
From the Day Room 148
The Leave Train 149

From *A Box of Silver Birch* (1997)
Noah Changes His Venue 150
In Reverse 151
The Terrible Beauty of Efficiency 152
Olivia (Aged Nearly Five) 153
Lament of a Twentieth Century Poet 153
'Happiness Writes White' 154
Retired 155
Suddenly It's Winter 156
Jeu d'Esprit 157
Loss of Grief 158
A Box of Silver Birch 158

PART TWO
POEMS FOR YOUNGER READERS

Sweet Music Is Not Only Drawn from Lute 160
Who and Why? 161
Hitting the Moon 162
The River Idle 163
Kingfisher 163
Dead Blackbird 164
Man Alive 165
The First Day of Spring 165
Heatwave 166
Fall 166
Sally 167
Ward F4 168

PART THREE
UNPUBLISHED POEMS

It's All Been Said Before 172
Not the Poem I Planned 172
Words in Waiting 173
What I Most Dislike 173
The Cage 174
lower case 174

The Third Day	175
Loss of Grief	176
The Old Song	176
On Putting the Clocks Back	177
Arrested	178
Portrait	179
The Wind's Way	180
The Death of Summer	180
Tidying Up	181
Return to Ribblesdale Place	182
20th Century Enlightenment	183
Terminus	184
Academic	185
Experts	186
Nameless	187
York Minster and St. Eadmer's	188
The Only Evergreen	189
Graveyard on a Hill	189
Reflections on Mortality	190
Reflections	190
Sundown	191
Blind Girl's Song	191
Reflection	192
What Is Nothing?	192
Credo 1	193
The Ballad of Two Stones	194
Winter Song	194
Poem	195
Every Situation Can Be Used to Advantage	195
No Score	196
Armchair Travel	196
Poem from My Wheelchair	197

PART ONE

PUBLISHED POEMS

Tom Rich

Tom Rich, the gardener,
has a strawberry mark on his face;
his hands are wide enough to span
the fattest vegetable-marrow.
With shirt-sleeves rolled,
forearm muscles swelled,
he pushes his comrade barrow to feed the roses.

In April he prunes each bush
deftly as a hairdresser
with skilful secateurs.
On the back of his hands the straw-gold hairs
glint amongst foxy freckles.
Now he is planting out
seedlings pale from long confinement
in the potting-shed:
the crooked, cumbrous fingers
approaching with gargantuan love
take each one gently as a dove
carrying home a feather to her nest.

Slowly he weeds the border,
his large boots
moving like careful barges near the roots
of coltness gem.
His giant shadow falls
where lilliputian ferns are waving
green signals to the butterflies:
cabbage-whites on dusty wings
zig-zag away, and booming bees
dizzying in-and-out of early flowers,
drugged with laburnum showers,
mumble in nectar-drunken drone
at his approach.

A caravanning snail with silver trail
removes its home to safety at the edge
of the strong box-hedge.
But not a violet need shield its head –
this grandson of Colossus
moves carefully as a deer
picking a dry-foot way among damp mosses.

Tom with his strawberry-face is rooted
strong as a tree in the garden.
And faithful like the robin
he never deserts
when the sundial's capped with snow,
but stays around, warming his hands and his dinner
at the outhouse fire,
throwing crumbs to the birds,
sharing their patience.

Lyric Evening

The afternoon closed around us like a witch
Grey-haired with rain.
In the twist of misshapen thorns we saw her nature
Spiteful and dark
Bent hunchback down to brush the rocky cheek
Of crags, with a withered kiss.
The harridan in rusty rags of bracken
Sat in a stone-grey huddle,
Chilled us in scarves of mist.

Then she leapt up and shrieked
Through crevices of deserted cottages –
No moss or fern could gentle that sawmill voice.
And she blocked our road gesticulating
With timber-creaking limbs until we fled
Her raw hill-weather fury.

But as we walked downhill together slowly
The evening rose to meet us like a lyric
With straight smoke from the valley,
And lights pricking their yellow stars
Through Winter-roughened larches.

St. Luke's Summer

Now is the tolling time
Between the falling and the buried leaf;
A solitary bell
Saddens the soft air with the last knell
Of Summer.
Gone is the swallow's flight, the curving sheaf;
The plums are bruised that hung from a bent bough,
Wasp-plundered apples in the dew-drenched grass
Lie rotting now.
Doomed with the rest, the daggered hawthorn bleeds
Bright crimson beads
For the birds' feast.
Gone are the clusters of ripe cherries,
Tart crabs, and damsons where the bullfinch tarried,
Only the camp-fire coloured rowan berries
Blaze on.
Now is the time of slow, mist-hindered dawns,
Of sun that stains
Weeds tarnished early in the chilling rains,
Of coarse-cut stubble fields
Where starlings gather, busy with the scant grain,
And with hoarse chattering proclaim
The spent season.
Now are the last days of warm sun
That fires the rusted bracken on the hill,
And mellows the deserted trees
Where the last leaves cling, sapless, shrunk, and yellow.
A robin finds some warm October bough
Recapturing his song
Of Aprils gone,
And tardy blackbirds in the late-green larch
Remember March.

The Tyrants 1942

Winter's ruthless horsemen ride
Steel-hooved across the pleading countryside;
Lanced with frost, and helmeted with snow
Onward they go
Cracking their whips among greying fields,
Spurred with death and armed with breakless shields.

Across the iron lake they ring,
Through petrified white woodlands echoing
Where flowers of brittle glass are cracked beneath
The hooves of death.
A metal vine twists from a frozen bough;
And every bearing tree is barren now.

All the sheltering birds have gone,
The stirring waves of Spring are caught in stone;
And swaying rushes stiffen into spears
Until one fears
That daffodils will never rise and blow
Their fluted triumph over fields of snow.

Between the Thought and the Word

This is the moment
Poised lightly between
The thought and the word raised above the earth –
When the Spring of a song
Beats a tune in the heart
Before the flood drowns it,
Roars over the deep inarticulate ring.

Before the tale's told
Or the bud a plain flower,
Before the black finger has measured its hold
On the hour –
These are the moments to capture and know.

Lovers, be slow,
Sheathe the bright words like dangerous swords,
Be wary as foxes,
Stealthy as snow.
Cover your joy with a crystal, a bell glass,
Shelter it, shield it, never breathe over it
Lest it should vanish
Like frost on the grass.

The Dipper

Here where the river is slender and small,
Tumbling like a child over stones in its fall
From pool to pool,
Here where the slant willow leans her breast
Over the secret of a dipper's nest,
The dipper himself stands all alone
Bowing to the river from his platform of stone.

How dapperly in black he bows with his back
To the strings in the stream,
And the sunlight-fingered harp
Touched into music on the sharp-edged stones,
To the bright trombones,
And the horns, and the flutes,
And the reedy clarinets whose woodland undertones
Murmur in the river from the alders at the edge,
From the rustle in the sedge.

How assuredly in white he bows from left to right
To the river where tiny-tendoned cresses
Are caught in weeds' caresses
In river traps of light.
And from his rocky rostrum the dipper bows, and blesses
Every river sound and sight.

The Pedlar

If Love, the pedlar, knocks upon your door
Begging for shelter, craving your heart's bread,
Think well before you let him in, or spread
A feast for his delight, lest he take more
Than you can spare, devouring your heart's store,
And you become the threadbare one instead,
Pleading that you may share his board and bed,
Imploring his bright wares for evermore.

Who lets in Love buys all his gifts with tears.
He takes your peace of mind for new desires
Till you become his slave and cannot rest
From serving him who tortures you with fears
Of loneliness, with dread of wasting fires
When he becomes the host and you the guest.

Search

I searched the crowded highway
For an answer I never found.
I wearied my soul aspiring
To stars, while myself was bound
In a house of clay. I hungered
For substance from shadows and dreams.

I followed the twisting river
To find the distant source that seems
Beyond the bend in eternal
Evasion of purpose and hope.
I clung to a lifeline of cobweb
But never of rope.

And love that I longed for and never
Could hold, is a ghost, for I find
Phantoms, and echoes whose footfalls
Inhabit my mind,
Turning away and returning,
Mocking my hopes, till their jeers
And reminders of failures are burning
And branding my ears.

But now for the first time dreamless
I wake, and with pain understand
I have wasted the richest years walking
And building on sand.
I climb unshod like a beggar
To the heights of a rock-paved land –
For hard to the feet is heaven
As granite is hard to the hand.

Northern Stone

Sap of the sullen moor is blood of my blood.
A whaleback ridge and whiplash of the wind
Stripping the branches in a rocking wood –
All these are of my lifestream, scoured and thinned.

Lack-leaf Spring, monotonous days of wet
And grudging acres where the sheep live hard;
Unfeatured country where no weed can set
A yellow eye to light reluctant sward;
The untamed fell, spreading a matted mane,
Gold as a lion below the dying sun,
And cat-o'-nine-tails of the scourging rain
Companion me when every friend has gone.

And now the grape-bloom of a night-blue hill
Surrounds my spirit with a deep content;
O, profligate with stars, the night is still
Regenerate of all that day has spent!

Lurks no concession in the northern stone
And stubborn soil and shock-haired tufts of reed?
The few who thrive here feed upon the bone;
None look for plenty in the famished seed.

Yet, breath of my breath, they have me by the throat,
These dark, indifferent moors that take no care
For life resurgent in the starving root
And love undaunted by the hostile air.

Giraffes

Beyond the brassy sun-stare where each shade
Crouches beneath its substance at mid-noon
The tall giraffes are gathered in a glade
Grazing the green fruit of the midday moon.
Patched with sienna shadows of the jungle
In pencil-slender attitudes they stand
Grotesque in camouflage, each curve and angle
Merged into the backcloth of the land.

Circus creatures of a poet's dreaming,
Secure on stilts they seldom need to run,
Keeping silent watch on the hunters' scheming,
Moving unseen, unheard, are swiftly gone.
Strange genesis in which the substance seeming
The shadow is the secret of the sun.

Zebras

When Day strode over undiscovered hills
Blinding the stars and rolling back the Night
From Chaos, a hidden generation heaved
Below the huge command: 'Let there be Light!'
In that stark union of black and white
The zebras leapt in earth's gigantic womb.

Now streaking over old sun-dazzled plains
In striped security, beyond the reins
Of man, they race unlassoed by his will.
Stubborn and shy and caged in comic bars
Of camouflage, they roam unbroken still.
Scorning the saddle and the dragging wheel,
They breed in freedom, tented by stars,
Unstabled, unharnessed, unled
By bit and bridle to domestic bed
And water from a bucket – what wild lake
Or river glistens in the zebras' eyes?
What elemental fountain leaps to slake
The thirst of these who feed upon the sky's
Enormous bounty?

The dull hoof-thunder of their destiny
Rolls through the generations saved from man
To live in liberty outside his plan
For breaking beauty to a sullen toil.
Compound of grass, sun, moon and soil
The zebras shun the world's stupidity.
Happier they than horses, donkeys, mules,
These wise ones, never tamed nor cajoled by man
Who breaks the hearts and then the backs of fools.

I Am Not Resigned

The will forbids; the heart has flown
Down long green tunnels overgrown
By arches leafed with memory.
Here's the brushwood pile: the wood,
The log-filled waggon; here we stood
And watched it creak downhill.
Blue puddles of inverted sky,
Blue smoke, blue haze, a curlew's cry
Come back and hurt me still.

The road goes where we cannot go;
Mist hides all we long to know.
Only the black lake frets and glooms
And fills the mind's deserted rooms
With images of yesterday.

A glen of shadows, hills where rise
Legends from greener centuries,
The house beside the lake, the lane
That leads the heart back home again –
All these invade my mind.
And though the bridges, stiles and streams
Remain, we cross them in our dreams;
And *I am not resigned.*

It Was Not I

There came a night I slept for hate of day,
Then followed days I feared to leave the night.
Reluctantly I faced the challenge: Light!
With shaking hands I shut the dark away:
Necessity stood naked on the brink
Of death – I clothed her hating every stitch
And longed to tread her helpless in the ditch
Where struggle dies and pride and purpose sink.

It was not I who waited on despair
Till misery became my comforter,
Or nursed paralysis to health until
I moved in spite of my reluctant will.
The motive was not mine that moulded pain
Into a cup that breaks and brims again.

Over the Water

In Spring I must return to secret places
Of greenhood by remembrance revealed
In swift unbidden flashes when lost faces
Smile back unharmed across a trodden field.
In Spring I must surprise the dwindling river,
Replenish it from this sharp source of tears
Confessing to the stream that love forever
Flows unsubdued beneath the bridge of years.

Beneath the bridge – I lean again and wonder
At water wrinkling down the tides of time;
A dipper finds a stone, a trout flicks under;
For one held moment heart and nature rhyme.
A willow stoops to finger its reflection,
And I am in the water and the tree
Where sunlight makes a shadow-world perfection
Put on the substance of reality.

Time has not betrayed the moving finger;
I turn back to the written page and look
And in a timeless statement live and linger;
The plot remains; age cannot cheat the book.
And though the coloured summers flame and topple
From torchlight trees to rustle underfoot,
And voices fade to echoes in the silence,
Spring rises in us from a deeper root.

Blue Tits

Bobbing on willow branches, blue and yellow,
Acrobatic blue tits swing and sway
In careful somersaults and neat gyrations
Grub-picking deftly down each bending spray.

Now one rebuffs an alien intruder –
Humdrum sparrow, drab among the gold,
Churrs and scolds in azure-crested anger,
Scuttles down a twig in blue and bold
Defiance at this urchin gutter-haunter
Till all the blues combine against one grey:
Active whirr and flutter, feathered thunder
Of tiny wings to drive the foe away.

Brave blue tit, white-cheeked like a painted toy
Jerking to life from pavement-seller's string,
Twirls round twigs, his natural trapezes,
Darts to snap a moth upon the wing.
Plump-as-willow-catkin, primrose-breasted,
This sky-capped morsel magnifies the Spring.

Nothing Grows Old

This is the hour the gods set to music:
Song in the branches, hope in the heart,
Rhythm in poplars like green spires adorning
The morning in tune with the moment apart.

Today is a soaring; and summit and steeple
And smoke from the clearing discover the sky.
Uncover the sky for us, upward-bound skylark –
The song will remain though the singer must die!

This is the peak of the measureless minute
That mankind aspires to and never can hold,
Disclosed in a flash by a primrose, a linnet –
The instant that tells us that nothing grows old!

The Old Lead Mines

This is a land of lead.
Grey deserted water denies all life below
a sullen gleam of pewter.
The ring of life is over:
no one works the stone.
The lead mines are grown over by uncouth rough
and tangle of nettle, briar and bramble.
A sheep, more like a stone than animal,
is grazing an unrewarding crevice.

This land is darkened, yet gorses snatch
a pittance from this impoverished country.
Reluctant Spring displays hidden fairings with hesitant
cold fingers flaring into a golden proclamation:
'Life is still a challenge!
The grasses here are blighted:
man sees, yet is benighted.'
The cold earth turns and grumbles:
a stricken oak tree, sheltered from the storm,
brings forth ochre wizened leaves that flutter
into Summer, and are gone.

This is a land of lead.
Sharp thorn trees scratch a living,
but the antlered oaks are dead.
This moor is a land where hope is unconfessed.
High among the heather-dark cradle of weather –
the many footed wind can never rest;
but brushes back the Summer,
bringing down the hammer
of hail upon Spring's half-opened door.
And Poverty stares, huge-eyed, on the moor.

Drought

The grey ground hardens like a beggar's crust;
And paper flowers, sucked of sappy stores
Are streaked with rust.
Yet one bass-booming bee explores
Warm lily lips, and crazed with honey lust
Clambers and slips within the wrinkled chalice.

The smouldering hive of Summer has run dry
For nectarous rain and juice beneath the skin.
The heat-dome dazzles between earth and sky,
And senses flog desire leashed within
The withered heart and unrewarded eye.

Send us a bulging sail of cloud to break
The torpor of this unrelenting blue,
Turn us towards the cold until we slake
Our thirst with rain and dew!
O storm, awake
And thrash the sulking rivers till they roar
Mouthing a tiger-foam in maddened race!
Call up the fountains from the earth's embrace
To spout like whales and rinse the dusty air.
Strike the adamant rock until rockfast rills
Burst from impotent loins of rigid hills!
Pump water from deep wells to ease our blood,
And drown us in a deluge to the sound
Of rain rods beating the breast of barren ground!

A Christmas Tree Speaks

No wind comes here to rock my rhythmic branches,
And sun and rain and soil are shut away –
They would destroy unseasoned tinsel splendour,
And snuff these candles with the breath of Day.

Now I must scintillate with brittle glory,
And scratch the ceiling with a paper star;
A plaster sky confines my Christmas story;
I cannot reach the mysteries that are
Hushed in the heart when outer fret and turmoil
Denies the peace that longs to come to birth.
But lives the Christ Child only in a carol?
Beyond a song, is there no peace on earth?

The Open Door

Cul-de-sac! The road begins for me
Beyond the broken gate across the lane.
In this brown wilderness my life is free
From narrow regulations that restrain
The searching heart, for here I can explore
Lost country of the mind as on I go
Across the barren fell, the open door
To all I loved and hoped for long ago.

The matted grasses, and the honey smell
Of white stone bedstraw, sweet amongst the sour,
The black bog water and the bright green dell,
Rain sodden acres, and the sudden flower
That swings from wiry harebell stalks – all these
Revive old memories till I am young
With dreams that wake in weather-toughened trees
And birds that speak a long-forgotten tongue.

Though hope has failed and doubt grown strong,
And truth revealed the changing mind's deceit,
There is a country where we all belong,
Where love springs deathless from the heart's defeat.
We do not pray on aching knees with minds
constrained to hold an errant thought or plea –
Our prayers are heard beyond all speaking:
Truth is told in silence that is stronger than the word.

Wordsworth's Old Age

Sunlight once played upon the granite ledges
Now shadowed by austerity of mind;
And from the place where primroses have rested
The warm earth has declined.
Cold is the rock face, moss and lichen banished
To green forgotten springs locked deep below
A frozen crust; the celandine has vanished.
Where star and violet shone now falls the snow.

You, the river brimmed with life reflecting
Forms and colours we could not perceive
Until you shone the mirror through our blindness,
Are now a dry bed where the willows grieve.

Can old age answer for a poet's dying?
(Those bony fingers pinch a shrinking flame.)
Or was it passion cold upon the anvil
That failed your sensual heart till no spark came
To startle innate iron with sudden glory
Transcending vulgar metal? Was it shame
Or sanctioned love that tamed your blue-hawk spirit,
Drugging the Muse with kindness and with calm,
And dropped domestic oil on seething torrents
To soothe such ecstasy with deadly balm?

You who wrote your name in rock and rainbow
And sang of summits till you dwarfed the earth,
Are now tight-lipped, ungiving as the gritstone,
Lodge for the bones where once a bird had birth.
When the heart is out no hearth-fire warms the poet;
To find a spark his will must strike on stone.
But stone is hostile to a tired spirit –
The poet is dead: a man lives on alone.

The Mallard

Brown-checked, neat as new Spring tweed,
A mallard, wing-stretched in the sun,
Watched from the bank of a beer-bubble stream
Her ducklings, one after one,
Daring, dipping in dazzling weed,
Nuzzling joyful mud.
Black and yellow, downy as bees,
They busied about a fringe of reed
In a paddled nursery pool.

The mother, content, lay dry,
Relaxed her wings, slackened her throat,
Dared to close one bead-black eye
When swift as terror a lightning stoat
Forked and flashed upstream.

Splatter and splash of mother and young –
Feathered drops whirled in a storm of fear,
Water thrashed in flight.
A stone for the stoat – I flung it near
And stood alone, not knowing what fate
Lay crouched in wait, while the stillness there
Grew ominous and bright.

Prayer for Sun

We cry for the sun
To come bright-clashing through these solemn clouds
That muffle every song in woollen shrouds
Grey-soaked with rain.

Let sunlight sweep across the hidden plain
That suffers in a rain flood, daisy deep,
Where lizards creep
For safety on stones, where birds complain,
And rabbits keep
To the hills because the Flood is here again!

Send forth Thy dove
With a sun-bright leaf
And we will learn that love shines through our grief.
We wait to see the elemental arch
Of water and of light
Bridge all the earth in seven-coloured span
Reminding man
Of a promised land beyond our human sight.

She

She is air and light –
Sun and moon and stars and loosened flame;
We are shadows dancing in her name.
She's quicksilver, a vein of gold
In ordinary day,
The play
Of leaves and ripples charged with energy.
She's wind and fire and darkness and desire,
Cymbal-clash and brush of thistledown,
Lightning-flash across the brain,
A spark struck out between
Cold iron and cold stone,
A sudden rainbow in a drop of rain.

Walking on Air

To see her walking down the street
Demurely, with her flying feet
Folded like birds in buckskin neat,
To watch her wait all willow grey
Against the wind within the sway
Of quaker skirts, who'd guess a gay
Green leprechaun slept deep in her?
For she can dance in dreams and stir
Plain city men to weep for her.

The street is drab, yet pennons fly
The way she goes, and when we try
To walk with her, she walks the sky.

Breath of All the World

This is the war of Head against the Heart
And Age, the surest ally fights for Head
With knowledge and experience outspread
To overwhelm the foe before the start.

And yet the impulsive Heart beats on –
A losing force against Reason's cold contempt.
Philosophy has won the battle:
The flame is blown out by the lips it taught.

Logic rules the world and lyrics fade
Bewildered by Platonic cannonade:
That life evolves by reason we can prove.
The Head commands, but not one voice replies –
The Breath of all the world is drawn by Love.

Snow

The wind's abed; the Winter sun
Is muffled in a wool of sullen cloud;
The moon is hid with all the stars
Pillowed in darkness while a shroud descends.

In a silent night of sleep the snow defends
A shivering world
Until blank day reveals in white amaze
The moors all furred,
A stone barn thatched and oak trees pearled;
All hollows rounded, all angles curved.
The blinded signpost points to unknown roads
Where all is capped, cloaked, clouded or concealed –
The substance mocked and transience revealed.

The metamorphosis refutes man's power.
What army could command
Such instant camouflage?
Or absolute surrender without a sound?

Midsummer

Brushing the stone paths with a sound of leaves,
Tom pursues the weeds with slow intent,
His whole will bent on a pile of dead Spring flowers
Smouldering in the Summer sun; sharp fires
Of Autumn are not kindled, and this smoke
Pale blue as lupin spires
Is sweet and lazy as the heat of June.
But Tom moves with careful industry –
No speed, no waste; potential energy
Is stored against the time for cutting down,
The time when thick delphiniums fall like corn,
And hope-high hollyhocks can flower no more,
When marguerites are trampled by the wind,
And only the circus dahlias wait behind
To blaze through hoops of death.

But now the year has climbed up to its height;
Each plant stands tiptoe with a weight of bloom;
Regret can find no room;
Desire is satiate; and Tom knows
The secret of repose lies hidden in the earth.

Now noon lies drowsing down the garden paths;
And the sundial casts no shadow
As Tom straightens from his morning task.
Midsummer and midday and life mid-way
Between the dark and dark, between two sleeps;
It seems like Light unveiled, a moment held
And nothing more to ask.

The Swifts

The swifts descend the twilight bends of air
Between dark beeches on this Summer night;
And looping up the dusk with bows of flight
They poise a moment pinioned breathless where
All movement is suspended in delight.

Then surging downward with their seed-pearl cries
They thread the night with ecstasy of sound
Till the listening earth is lifted to the skies,
And the arch of night comes curving on the ground.
Swept to a peak of air on mating wing
They pin us to a pinnacle of joy
Where vanished petals of a fallen Spring
Unfold beyond all power to destroy.

In Praise of Darkness

Maternal darkness wraps my mind in peace,
For darkness is the cradle of the earth
And curtains aching light from infant eyes –
Dark is the womb that brings a star to birth.

Darkness is my comfort and my friend –
Knowledge that change must be towards the light;
Darkness is the inn at the world's end;
Strong arms to fold the tired day with night.

Dark was the hour that heard the first command:
'Let there be light!' Obedient darkness fled
To be a backcloth for the rising land,
A foil for stars that glittered overhead.

Darkness takes my hand when lamps confound
My journey down this labyrinth of days.
Out of the dark I came to search all ways;
Into the dark I go where light is found.

Integration

The undertow is strong tonight, my love;
Throughout the day my harnessed forces row
Against the tide, but now the unsleeping flow
Omnipotent has swept me to your side.

My little boat, fragile among the reeds
Of circumstances, created for the needs
Of man to cross the straits of loneliness,
Is tugged two ways; and I must ride the stress
Where heart and head are crossed waves on the tide.

Face to the shore, I haul my will to land;
There is no helm that reason cannot turn.
Only the kick of a wave diverts my hand;
And a star can sting and burn.

The will must rest; and now I am ashore,
A Nothing upon a bank of sleep, whose soul
Unknowing has drifted where itself is known.

Skeleton Bride

I come to you now to woo your mind
(Because your heart is dead)
Stripped of defence that you may find
New pleasures for the head
In my chaste and calcined tread.

See how my ribs let the moonlight in!
Feel the sockets of my eyes –
Each one pockets a star; I grin
For you may not chastise
Responses of the flesh, the bloom
Of shoulder, cheek, and breast;
The cramped cell of your mind has room
To give a skeleton rest
And still be unpossessed.

I come not to possess or claim
A handshake or a glance;
I come to challenge a living shame
With death's revealing dance
That flings the concealing veils aside –
All seven on the floor –
To strip me naked, heaven's bride,
Till now I stand before
Your gaze, a woman no more.

O won't you test my rigid wrist
And fingers pencil-fine?
Explore the mouth where once you kissed
Your soul away in mine?
And come and take me now dissolved
Of every warm desire –
Each curve and cave and clasping limb
Resolved in Arctic fire?

Fastidious and proud, you may
Remain in your embrace
Remarking the intricate way
My bones fit into place,
Glad that I have no face,
No force to pull your soul away
From gravity to grace.

Imagination

The primrose shape was printed on His mind
Before the primal dawn, before the springs
And rivers gathered from imagined rain;
Before the earth was made He knew all things.

Darkness cannot blind the eyes of light
To every creature's form, before the seed
Forests of sound and colour fill His sight;
Imagination generates the deed.

Darkly in a glass the shadows move
And in the dark we see our human race
Reflected from the archetype of Love,
And dare to dream the hidden *face to face*.

John Clare Dreaming

Midday is a golden bell-tent strained
From daisy pegs by indecisive wind
When a tired farm-hand, cherishing the hour,
Creeps through the flap, furtive as a thief.
Beyond command, his large and patient hands
Are freed from iron of the tyrant spade.
Floating down the ebb of consciousness
He drowns beneath receding waves where sleep
Releases him, draws off his clumsy boots . . .

In sleep a king . . .
With stockinged feet I tread the royal wheat;
Down leisured sovereign waterways I glide,
My barge obedient to the purple tide
That bears my dust away.
Seven swans in skein unwind the sheets
Long folded on a shelf above my reach;
Ermine and swansdown clothe my country clay.

In sleep a king . . .
Till through the haze I hear the drowsy bees
Brushing the gold-dust from my dreams; I wake
To farmyard stir and clatter,
And stumble through the fields with jabbing rake
Tearing apart my ragged bed of clover.

In sleep a king, but waking no such matter.

Spring in a City

Spring takes the street today;
The fields are sweet
Where the high trees catch her song as she goes by.
But higher than the trees her heart pursues
Chimneys and spires – she holds them and imbues
The people passing with a leaf-edged mood.

Green footed on a pavement, here she stands
Behind a barrow-load of flowers: the dust
Of old beginnings breathed on once again
Becomes a bunch of violets in her hands.

Geraniums Are Verbs

From this white bed I dream of coloured days
When I could feel my limbs and dance and run
Away from the school room where the passive red
Of blackboard verbs grew active in the sun.

But now geraniums in my window box
Can knot my heart round with the scarlet sash
Of petalled velvet from dancing frocks –
Geraniums are verbs because they flash
The ball of childhood from a Summer park
Into this ransomed life till I can watch
The daylight dwindle to a dazzling dark.

For brightness beads my dreams, and crippled limbs
Grow straight and swift as deers' and children's are;
Beauty is twisted by a lie that dims
Before the truth of one recurring star.

My life is rooted like these flowers that teach
Beyond all books what knowledge cannot know;
They fill my hands with beauty out of reach –
I travel though I may not rise and go.

Geraniums are verbs because they bring
Action into the stillness I must keep –
A stillness of the soul that learns to fling
Aside the covers of this mortal sleep.

I Have Not Seen God

I have not seen God face to face
Therefore I cannot fear him.
But I fear lightning and the anger of righteous men,
And this grasping at space
In a night grown huge behind trembling stars.

I have not seen God face to face
Therefore I cannot worship him.
But I worship mountains that wear a bloom of grapes
In the evening sun; I worship primitive things –
Trees and essential shapes
Of beauty outlines in the world we touch.

I have not seen God face to face
Therefore I cannot love him.
But I love the light that quickens wood and stone,
The sudden grace
Lifting a dull pedestrian out of time
And place, to find the unknown in the known.

A Poem in an Old Man's Heart

I have become a poem
Grown in an old man's heart;
Compound of memory and dreams I sprout
Like an unsown wand of wheat.
Inviolate is the unsown that never can be reaped
Save in the golden reaches of the mind
Shielded from frost, beyond the bullying wind
That bends the striving human corn to earth.

I push aside the flag-stones of his world
To flower in perfection of a dream.
Potential truth and beauty lie uncurled,
Unbruised in that projection of himself
He once mistook for me.
For he snares his image in a net of words
Till a phantom puts on flesh
And trapped reflection becomes reality.

In Silverwell Street

She sweeps the steps of Silverwell Street
In a tulip red dress;
And brushing with rhythmic stress
She holds the broom in strong caress,
For work is nature in Silverwell Street.

Her hips are neat
Like a folded tulip on delicate stem
As she bends to the dust in humble grace;
With down-bent face
She sweeps the flags beneath men's feet.

But no man sees her graceful act
For all are troubled by fear or fact.
Obsessed, oblivious they pass
And leave the Spring behind
Where stones are cool to the feet as grass
And a tulip sways in the wind.

The dust flies around in the April air
And flaps her skirt and twists her hair
And flutters the frills around her throat.
But the people passing up and down
Are wrapped in care and are unaware
That Spring has opened a flower in town.

The Buttercup Children

Down the dusty lane of Summer
Thick with scent, tangled with honeysuckle,
The children come so slowly
You'd think the afternoon would lie for ever
Sleeping along the hedges without shadow.

School is the past; tomorrow is only a name,
And sorrow has no share in this enchantment.
They live in the immediate delight
Of butterflies and clocks of dandelion
Blown as soon as looked at, without time
To jostle them from one thought to another.

Theirs is the present
Wide open as a daisy to the sun;
They do not bruise it in their gathering.
What though these shining buttercup bouquets
Droop in their eager hands?
The gold ungrudging petals drop behind
Uncounted through a timeless afternoon.

House in the Tree

The house in the tree now tenanted by the wind
Was once your hiding-place –
Green-foot, goat-foot, you leapt above earth;
Each day I see your face
Laughing between leaves, mocking at care.

This leaning ladder beckons you again
To windy roof-tops where you found the sun.
Neither the slant rain
Nor the grey wolf-hollow wind
Could daunt your coloured escapades.

Yours was a rainbow mind
Of sudden come-and-go,
Winking through trees like water,
Vanished like the puff of a dandelion-clock.
I see you now
Gazing enraptured at the year's first snow,
Pranking through fields with a butterfly-net.

You discovered a world that was gay
With zig-zag butterflies and feathered snow,
Crack of bonfires and the polished bay
In prickly chestnuts, handkerchiefs stained red
With blackberry juice.
Days were coloured beads upon a thread
Each one brighter than the one before.

Now, no sound,
No dizzy wheels flashing, scorning the ground –
Your circus bicycle is shut away
With rust and cobwebs that you never knew.
Yet on a Summer night that smells of hay
When the screeching barn-owl tears the years away
I find you again
Asleep in your tent, untouched by the prowling dark
And the difficult joy grown strong through living with pain.

The Fox

It was twenty years ago I saw the fox
Gliding along the edge of prickling corn,
A nefarious shadow
Between the emerald field and bristling hedge
On velvet feet he went.

The wind was kind, withheld from him my scent
Till my threaded gaze unmasked him standing there
The colour of last year's beech leaves, pointed black,
Poised, uncertain, quivering nose aware
Of danger throbbing through each licking leaf.
One foot uplifted, balanced on the brink
Of perennial fear, the hunter hunted stood.

I heard no alien stir in the friendly wood,
But the fox's sculpted attitude was tense
With scenting, listening, with a seventh sense
Flaring to the alert; I heard no sound
Threaten the morning; and followed his amber stare,
But in that hair-breadth moment, that flick of the eye,
He vanished.

And now, whenever I hear the expectant cry
Of hounds on the empty air
I look to a gap in the hedge, and see him there
Filling the space with fear; the trembling leaves
Are frozen in his stillness till I hear
His leashed-up breathing – how the stretch of time
Contracts within the flash of re-creation!

Bleasedale; the Wooden Circle

The Wooden Circle at Bleasdale and that at Woodhenge are believed to be the oldest in Britain (circa 1400 B.C.). The wooden stumps from Bleasdale, now in Preston Museum, are the only ones still in existence.

In the sun of a late Summer I return
To the land where I was born –
The true magnetic North with its dark moods
And heather-shouldered fells where the green corn
Delays the farmers' year.

Here is the stream that washed our youth away
Under the bridge's eye,
And the black unblinking pond, thick-lashed with reeds,
That gazes at but never holds the sky.

This country is dynamic, beckoning
Her sons back to the stormy solitudes
And tawny marshes where reluctant Spring
Retards the leaf; vitality unspent
Is leashed within the acorn and the bud.
And in these brooding silences between
Age-twisted oaks and bristled firs there breathes
A spirit older than the ageless earth.

A shawl of sun surrounds the infant church
That of itself can give back merely shadows
From stones that gave it birth.
But the soul of man was born when he stood up
From dust to gaze in wonder at the sun.
After the seedless silences of cold
He looked to the east and saw his golden god
Risen from nowhere to subdue the night.

Time falls away; unmeasured ages wheel
Through ice and stone and bronze till now we stand
On the circle where our fathers sang to the sun.
Here priest and peasant have stood
In the first prayer facing towards the east.
And wonder, ever young, still gropes behind
The sun for motive, feels the muscled wind
And questions whence it came.

Reclaimed

A fallen star
Cooled from the sun to the brink of death we are
Till Love awakes and warms us into life.

Stiffened waves relax and curl around
Untrodden shores, exploring empty caves;
Fish flicker into life and flash upstream;
The long grey dream
In stony river-beds is broken by
Water thrashing down a mountain-side.
A rigid forest stirs towards the sun,
Lets forth its birds like some old falconer
Forgetful of his art
Till memory informs his frozen brain
That Pan is here; the world is green; and all
The ache of living – beauty spiked with pain –
Begins again.

Branches cradling the wind
Shake out pink-fisted blossom; crumpled leaves
Expanding in the light unclose
The blue forget-me-not, the first wild rose
Pale as a shell from centuries of cold.
And man and woman, gazing upon these,
Rejoice in freedom of the hills and seas
But by their need for love themselves are bound;
And each surrenders wholly to the other.

Such union cannot hold;
Not only trees but lovers must grow old
And die.
Fear creeps around them; Death comes near to try
Their wholeness with his dark dividing rod –
And there's no hiding-place from his huge eye.
Like drowning men they reach out for a god
Imploring him to listen and to save.

There is no shelter in the toppling wave,
No warmth in the opening cave,
No consolation in the thought of Truth,

Goodness and Beauty without human form.
Only a man can understand their need
And serve them as a god.
Pan with his goat-legs has escaped, and fills
The air with wordless echoes and a sound
Of laughter that intensifies the wound
Of separation.

Only a man, mortal as ourselves,
Wearing our clothes, sharing our daily food
Can clear the brambled path for our return.
A carpenter drives nails into the wood
Towards the day when gathering beads of blood
Shall shine like rowan-berries from his wrists.
But now the footpath twists
From light to dark, and truth half-understood
Fades from the desperate mind; the unguarded heart
Cries out in terror at its loneliness.
A mist comes down and all is blind again.

Where is the promised moment of return
To more than Eden when we played half-grown
Like children in the sun?
We've searched the planets, lost ourselves to find
Our faces in the mirror staring back
The eternal question that has no reply.

A fallen star
Cooled from the sun to the brink of death we are
Till Love awakes and leads us into life.

Recapitulation

Whenever I return
Anchorless to that harbour
Where the grey houses in the grey rain
And the poppy-coloured boat out in the bay
Are branded on my brain, I meet you on the quay –
In the tea-shop with its windows to the sea
Framed in a foam of lace.

Through the mist and the half-sun
Dropping on golden gardens and the bronze
Bitter chrysanthemums,
Again I see your face.

And while my unaware companion
Babbles of boats and birds,
I'm caught away from words; the holiday place
Escapes me in my errant capturing
Of thoughts on wing, a mood that backs away,
A form, half-shadow – how a slant of light
Plays on these known surroundings like a tune
That recapitulates.

Love Without Frontiers

To have met you and loved you and not to have stayed
Till footsteps dragged and lark-music delayed
Its ascension,
To have left on the up-beat and not to have known
The end of surprise,
To have kissed and departed and wept and grown wise
In knowledge of love – by this we are made
Immortal, inviolate: none can invade
A love without frontiers that sees without eyes,
Is present in absence and never denies
The unexplored country beyond.

Evergreen

The language of life is green
And in this tongue I send you messages.
Although we may not meet, the way between
Is leafed with words; meaning unfolds and grows
Through white and leafless silences that lie
Bare as the Winter of expectancy.
Not dead but sleeping – this much knowledge knows:
Hope is an evergreen that dare not die.

The Vine

All my fruit is yours for you are mine,
The root and stem from which my tendrils twine;
You are the warmth that swells my tender grapes.

My leaves are hands uplifted to your light;
Each palm grows bright to catch the falling sun.
And when the waiting nets of night
Are wide to hold earth's ripeness we are one –
Root, branch, and leaf and rounding fruit begun
In life's full circle.

White root, go deep
That in your tunnelled darkness I may sleep;
Strong branch, reach high
Till my green hands, glad servers of the sun,
Receive the cup of water and of fire
And find it brimmed with wine –
I drink you, drain you till my life in yours
Is yours in mine.

Village Postman

Through sun and rain he rides his royal bicycle
Making downhill of the miles where we have trod;
Skimming the morning on his scarlet Pegasus.
He's winged and wheeled, half mortal and half god.

Our village Mercury, anonymous, discreet,
Sphinx-like above those flying handlebars,
Blue-shouldered, solid, without feathers on his feet
Though destiny has named him with the stars.

A sack of messages makes him a god,
An oracle – what dread and what delight
Leap up to hear his knock, what weighted hopes
Crash as he whistles past and out of sight!

Some watch for him at windows, some from under doors
Find overdue accounts, but none enquire
If that blue uniform is proof against
Arrows of anguish sharpened with desire.

Ploughing

At the field's edge
The chestnut mare with drooping underlip
Stands tail-in to the wind.
Her rusty coat is ragged as the bracken
For no one troubles her now
With harness for the hay-cart or the plough.

But see, along the hedge the bumping tractor
Puffing its blue smoke in the rain-cold air,
Bright as a toy-shop model it rattles along
Raising the furrows to its metal song.
Dark rows of chocolate corduroy are laid
Against the diminishing green – no horse-plough skill
Could turn the grass-side under with city speed.
The stubborn and unprofitable field
Will yield its sloping thigh to the strong machine
And lie through the Winter waiting for the seed.

Harlequin

Beyond the junk-shop of the mind
There lies a curtained inner room;
Here the hurt soul, unconfined,
Can breathe again and touch a bloom
Unbruised by grasping hands outside.
Take off your shoes, bring nothing in;
Fold your costume, harlequin –
The masquerading self has died.

Heron

On lonely river mud a heron alone
Of all things moving – water, reeds, and mist –
Maintains his sculpted attitude of stone.
A dead leaf floats on the sliding river, kissed
By its own reflection in a brief farewell.
Movement without sound; the evening drifts
On Autumn tides of colour, light, and smell
Of warm decay; and now the heron lifts
Enormous wings in elegy: a grey
Shadow that seems to bear the light away.

Fisherman Poet
(For Herbert Palmer)

He was farouche
with grey moustache,
an otter's look in his wild brown eyes
as he hooked a trout;
a wolf's snarl in his anger
flaring for a fight.

Yet he loved his adversary,
scourging weather;
chose to fish upstream;
unswerving will
followed the curving river to its source
in bed of rock,
bristle of heather.

There he mocked
flat, felted poets;
dim, grey speech down-toned
to pavements made him howl.

When no one listened
he sang to the wind – loud
songs till the larches bowed.
He cried to the stars,
nailed his meaning to the mast
of the tallest pine in the forest.

The stars opened their ears;
the wind's thong lashed;
but no one hears
his true song
now the wind has lain down
with otter and wolf,
and the poet on an island of reeds
returns to himself.

Death of a Gardener

He rested through the Winter, watched the rain
On his cold garden, slept, awoke to snow
Padding the window, thatching the roof again
With silence. He was grateful for the slow
Nights and undemanding days; the dark
Protected him; the pause grew big with cold.
Mice in the shed scuffled like leaves; a spark
Hissed from his pipe as he dreamed beside the fire.

All at once light sharpened; earth drew breath,
Stirred; and he woke to strangeness that was Spring,
Stood on the grass, felt movement underneath
Like a child in the womb; hope troubled him to bring
Barrow and spade once more to the waiting soil.
Slower his lift and thrust; a blackbird filled
Long intervals with song; a worm could coil
To safety underneath the hesitant blade.
Hands tremulous as cherry branches kept
Faith with struggling seedlings till the earth
Kept faith with him, claimed him as he slept
Cold in the sun beside his upright spade.

He Saved Others . . .
(for A.E. Rayner, Pioneer in Radiology)

He's in the dark-room again
reaching up with schoolboy elation
to examine the dripping plates –
ribs, femur, pelvis.
Here's a beautiful gall-stone
sharp against shadow,
and this obscene bud
swelling in honeycomb cells.

Faithfully the reel unwinds; he looks
into himself
having nurtured for years the avaricious flower
expanding in his entrails,
thrusting roots and petals through a vital part.

Without hope from the start
they tied up the bowel, made
makeshift with his guts,
massaged his heart,
fed him oxygen and blood.

From his hot white tent
he peers at us faraway children, struggles to reach
out and save, but the rope of speech
frays in twitching fingers.
He slips back into a whispering valley,
groping for a ledge of comfort.

Plucking the bedclothes, suddenly he jerks his head,
clutches iron rails from a gulley of pain,
scrabbles for a handhold, a jutting rock
on which to belay his life.

Geriatric Ward

Feeding-time in the geriatric ward;
I wondered how they found their mouths,
and seeing that not one looked up, inquired,
'Do they have souls?'

'If I had a machine-gun,' answered the doctor,
'I'd show you dignity in death instead of living death.
Death wasn't meant to be kept alive.
But we're under orders
to pump blood and air in after the mind's gone.
I don't understand souls;
I only learned about cells
law-abiding as leaves
withering under frost.
But we, never handing over
to Mother who knows best,
spray cabbages with oxygen, hoping for a smile,
count pulses of breathing bags whose direction is lost,
and think we've won.

Here's a game you can't win –
one by one they ooze away in the cold.
There's no society forbidding
detention of the old.'

The Dark Side of the Moon

Twenty hundred and twenty-five:
Freedom from need to stay alive.
This man-machine can think and act
More clearly; matter sticks to fact
And metal makes no claims; each part
Works perfectly without a heart.

No woman made grotesque with child –
The Super-Incubator smiled
On trays of re-conditioned eggs:
'We're going to breed 'em without legs –
They've moved around so long on wheels.
Our product neither sees nor feels
And wastes no time, and if it tires
We raise the voltage, change the wires.
No need for clothing, beds, or food
In dehydrated man, no crude
Relationships to reproduce
Obedient creatures for our use.
Metal and brain have long combined
Over the old illusion, Mind,
For we have found the reason Why
Behind the curtain of the sky.

The dark side of the moon is ours
Forbidden to men and beasts and flowers –
A foolproof Eden in the plan
To substitute our image for man.
We, the machine-gods without breath,
Have conquered time and space and death.'

Dilemma

As he lay dead,
frost-blue eyes hooded,
he looked like a Viking chieftain.
Grey-headed with strength and wisdom,
he needed no helmet or sword –
centuries slumbered in his folded arms.

They robed him in white;
and we were silent in his presence
listening for commands.
When fire had transformed
oakwood, roses, flesh, to ashes
we held the casket bewildered.
He had two wives;
and the dead wife was our mother;
but the widow cried, 'Scatter
them in the wood where he met me!'

Under the oaks, sowing, we paused,
dust on our hands:
'Let us divide him
as life divided him ...'
So we emptied half on our mother's grave.
And no voice came from the yew tree
to question and condemn.

The Palomino

The filly was rough in heather, free as the moor
Where she was bred, and grew
Ragged, rust red like the bracken.
Priding the herd with silver mane,
Tail of thistledown-silk,
She was promise too rare to let go –
A palomino, born to jump through hoops,
Bow to kettledrum and cymbal.

Eluding guile and ropes, she would not be driven
Into a corner of defeat.
Snuffing the wind, she sensed their booted approach,
Poised, a knifed second, on hind legs,
Flicked her head and plunged –
Into their knotted cordon.

It was bit and bridle; the long rein;
Paces tamed in perpetual circle;
Action trained, obedient
To steely hand and eye: relentless pivot
Of her roundabout world.
When frost grew bones in the earth
Clouds gathered in tent-folds
As she waltzed round a barrel in the spotlight,
Pom-poms trembling at the master drum.
The measureless moor became a red carpet
Felting her rhythmic hooves.

They wound her to clockwork perfection,
Brushed her mane to spun-glass,
Burnished their star
Performer, and were proved right
In backing this pliable-as-grass,
More than equine
Hobby-horse.

Seed Time

A sower went forth sowing.

And some fell in a test-tube,
Was conveyed by sterile glass to cold conception
In a warm and yearning womb,
Took root, grew from a loveless bed,
And knocked on the door of the world.

And some fell among flagstones
And straightway sprang from the cracks,
But lacking breath
Could not withstand the bruising, hurrying feet.

But one seed fell upon an open mind
And lay alone, as dead.
Imagination's coloured rain
Filled the dry corn, whitened it to bread.

Beginning

Beginning is
manifold, nameless
pulsing under sand;
breath
expanding folded lungs
in water, land, trees,
blowing blue winds
over mountains, seas;
mouth in dumb moss
speaking wild flowers,
singing leaves into birds,
sucking sinew and horn from heaving swamp,
whirling dust and rain
till footprints name untrodden sand.
Earth, maternal, groans
swinging aside the sea's blanket.
Beginning is
movement, sound, word.

Rise . . .

Summer lies thick along the hedgerows
foaming with chervil
splitting pods and spilling seeds
knees up in the grass, roses in her hair –
fertility act without statistics
or morals, buttons or zips
hindering fulfilment.

Alone for the first time
I walk among Summer's exuberance
shoes pollen-dusted
idly scattering rusty sorrel beads
in concert with the season.
June's hot hand in mine
I swish through plumy meadows to the water
watch moor-hens' bawdy sport among the reeds
where the lake flaps content.
A trout lies shallow, frilling fins and tail;
two butterflies still damp from birth
flicker in heat of a first and last day.
And the warm rise of Summer
sweats under my skin.

And Fall

Why am I sad?
It is Autumn;
leaves fall;
sun reddens early behind the hill.

Somewhere I hear
lifts going down,
lights clicking on
and feet hurrying home like leaves.

The Horses

Between waking and sleep
I am alone in a bright field
drifting towards a closing gate.
The gap narrows and I reach for the latch
but the black stallion arches through
trampling pale hems of dreams.
Nostrils, eyes sparking the darkness,
he is rubbed ebony at my thighs
lifting me along where I dare not go.

I left his bridle in daylight;
without reins I
melt in his muscled stride
across unseen land: no root or stone
hindering flight,
no turn for home in this curving ride.
Did we leap the gate
landing safe on the far side
with will absolved from need to fight
the dazzling dark?

Time broke with a blackbird singing
sharp as a star
nailing truth home.
It was a journey of splintered hooves
and black miles back to the field
and the white mare waiting at the gate
in first light.

I Give Death to a Son

Rhythmic pincer-jaws clench
and widen – the world explodes –
I give death to a son.
Tearing apart the veil he comes
protected fish from dark pool.
I push him over the weir,
land him on dry stones.

Was he anything, anywhere
behind, beyond
out there in nothingness?
Is he nothing, made aware
of cold, hunger, nakedness?

Trailing glory and slime
he is washed and dried,
grave-clothes ready warmed
by the fireside.

Boy Drowning

Drowning is pushing through
a barrier like birth
only the elements are exchanged:
air for water.
Then, water for air,
my lungs
folded flat as butterflies' wings
struggled to expand
in a round scream.

Now I make no sound –
or they don't hear
water damming my ear-
drums, nostrils, eyes –
I fight like a salmon on grass
choked with a bubble.
I cannot rise
a third time.

Cross

He was thorn
pierced through my flesh,
twisting away from earth's pull,
planets' rhythm.
In twitching limbs
dance was contorted;
speech leered from his mouth,
salivating words.

Hourly he beat me
with compassion's knobbed stick;
I swallowed resentment
like hairs.
My cupped hands
spilled pity's grit-in-the-eye.

Now he is gone
respite I longed for
sours the tongue.
Silence accuses;
peace whispered through grasses
dies on the wind.
Huge emptiness
engulfs my stand.
He was the cross
I leaned my life upon.

Old Corinth

The market-place at Old Corinth
has given up its fruits to time.
Roman pavements burn under our feet;
dry flowers rattle like paper as we pass.
We dare not dip into Peirine dripping ferns;
the guide beats us on.
Here St. Paul stood in the same sun
that strikes Apollo's temple
making all gods one.

The museum hums with many tongues –
swarming bees around Nero's head.
Escape is the courtyard leaf-and-sun
mosaic under a lemon tree.
History breathes from honeyed stone.

I hardly noticed his coming
so quietly beside me.
'May I share your shade?'
he said,
a pact already made
between two lovers of Greece.

We leaned back into centuries
turning wheels through oleanders, olive-groves,
turning helmets of bronze
where swords sheared the wheat till corn and blood
dropped thick to earth.
Wordless we gathered the harvest alive
shining beyond glass cases and confusion.

Museum

The word 'museum'
puts my soul into plaster of Paris.
Transfixed by B.C. flints,
moulded to Bronze Age bowls,
my eyes glaze at pottery
fired before earth was round.
I am broken on the wheel –
lapsed Catherine who cannot illuminate
past marvels with present wonder.
History clamps me in iron,
boots me with lead,
and there are stones in my handbag
too heavy to lug around gazing
on monoliths.
In this I am alone.
Around me are rapt crowds
silent as monks,
eyes, lips, mobile with praise;
vested in mystery they pass
velvet-footed from room to room.

I slip away
through a south door into the sun.
Breathing light and leaves
I revive like a tree
whose frosted armoury loosens in blossom.

Brief Encounter

No flowers, please, in plastic hoods –
This will not happen again;
Death's dark angel briefly broods
Indifferent to the rain

And briefly opens velvet wings
Upon the final scene
To fold them in the nick of time –
The coffin glides between.

A clockwork requiem fades out;
We rise up from our knees
Bewildered, and can almost hear
A whispered: *Next one, please.*

The 'crem' conveyer-belt slides on
From this world to the next
And everlasting Spring and sun
According to the text.

O, fire, is this thy victory –
Eternal sun and Spring
And truth reduced so tactfully
That Death has lost his sting?

I Cannot Look into the Sun

In your green anorak
flickering between the trees
I see you, gentle hob-nailed ghost,
a sack of logs on your back
bending towards the sunset.

In truth, I am the ghost
searching under a pile of Summer
for a buried axe.

Everything was lost those last days
when we lost each other –
I tried to hold you back in the dark wood
but a blackbird sang in your head
songs I never understood
whistling you away from clocks and signposts
up a path I could not follow.

Came Autumn with binding brambles
and blinding leaves
mocking map and compass.
When Winter divided us
I opened the book of rules
and heard Spring laughing at the lych-gate
where shadows change hands with light.

Can you see me wintering in the dark?
I cannot look into the sun.

Preparing to Leave

Attics cleared; shelves and drawers emptied;
Love-letters burned and memory purged,
I knew we had always been
Preparing to leave.
Those wedding-groups, snaps of childhood,
Babyhood, parents – back, back
To the unremembered, thrust
Deep into the dustbin.
The lid clashes louder than the Bible
That life is grass;
Possessions rust;
And man a moment of hope
From centuries' dust.

I walk out into wet fields of Spring;
Plovers are circling,
Crying to the rain and the trees,
Calling their young from empty nests –
Even these
Are pulled away on the swirl and heave
Of the wind.
All things that live are preparing to leave.

The Meths Men

Close to Strangeways Prison in Nightingale Street, Manchester, you may see, any time you pass, a group of destitute men just sitting there, drinking their lives away in surgical spirits.
(Extract from The Listener*)*

A short spit from Strangeways
the Meths Men
huddle together in Nightingale Street.
Rejects among rubble and rosebay
they're doing time
escaping from themselves
drinking day into night into day.

Behind chimneys the moon's cold eye
stares down; they don't look up
except with eyes shut,
bottle lifted in dummy comfort.

In Winter
spit freezes; they shuffle
into the Hostel of the Morning Star.
Last Christmas one chap wouldn't budge,
next day couldn't –
hair frozen to ground.
He was only half-dead
so they took him to hospital
and made him half-alive.

Immortality is a long word
and surgical spirit is slow.
Here is no fox's life, red to the death.
In Nightingale Street
dust creeps into mouths and minds.
They die grey.

Journey

I have died many times –
every night and every morning when
I leave the unknown darkness
where most I am alive
seeing shapes and colours never seen by day.

I died with my mother and my father –
and the roof was blown off my world.

Summers and winters drifted by
till the snow was a white cherry
shaken outside my window.
A blackbird whistled the world awake
and my son to be born in Autumn
quickened as I stepped on the first daisies.

There was singing in the sap
that ended in his green death
playing by the river.
Then I was a hollow as a wren's egg
blown by a schoolboy,
coming to life only in the green darkness
where his tent was pitched
under the willow.

One night he took my hand
telling of my journey over land and water
beginning again,
and he spoke to my daughter before birth.

Again the cherry and the blackbird,
falling leaf and snow
in magic circles
till she grew out of me –
more surely than being born –
when I'd grown into her,
made her life my own.

For that I had to suffer
a hard season of no growth
pruned low below the sunrise.
But life holds, draws, pulls
after light has gone
till the hidden flower opens
reaching for the sun.

What Is God?

I have not seen God face to face –
How can I love Him
whose answers to my questions are
silences in stone and star,
whose presence is my loneliness?

Incomprehensible Three-in-One,
how can I love Thee,
One-in-Three?

I love ordinary people
touchable, fallible
speaking my own tongue.

I love the real sun
whose warmth I feel
in whose light I live.
I love the green sap rising
from darkness into apple,
ape and man
becoming breath, mind, spirit –
invisible, intangible
three in one.
I love the mystery
that has no name.

Letter to Vincent

You never painted this picture, Vincent –
sunflowers pressed white on window-glass
by fingers of ice
beyond Summer skills of brush and knife.
No blood in these petals
shrinking under the sun.
No gold for our looking,
only evidence of cold, unhuman magic
that even you,
painter of poems without words,
have no colours for.

Call of the North

We rebuilt our childhood, leaf by leaf,
that bright day snatched from summers half-forgotten
half-remembered –
the Brock running brown under bridges,
the badger at home
and a dipper with golf-ball breast
bobbing on glistening stone.

We followed the river
up lost paths, over gates and stiles
broken by the years,
past the farm whose cherry in Spring
was white as their Lancashire cheese
to Delph crossroads where the beagles met.

D'you remember the long-legged hares,
tawny as rushes, with flattened ears,
racing in circles round Peacock Hill?
And Spring, green-tongued,
shouting 'Cuckoo'! over Sullom's shoulder
through days alight with gorse and finches' wings?

Here Bleasdale, damson-blue, bristled with heather,
sweeps north
from the slow slope of Fairsnape taking the sun,
ageless as wind and stone.

This country calls us back by roots
deeper than oak and birch,
darker than blood
to a land of belonging.
And always the river
that washed our youth away
runs on and runs forever.

Joie de Mourir

Look at me – I was a man once
walking upright
where this stone leans.
Read me: my name is William Brown
Aged seventy years
At Rest –
there your guess is wrong.

Certainly no talking here
or walking on grass –
it's we who leave you in peace
going about our own business
unshouldering the years.
I am ageless, untiring.
And Agnes, the twelve-year-old on my left,
is taller than the granite cross
you imagine her under.

The soldier on my right
went to the war –
only half of him returned.
His widow wept
over the man-sized box in the ground.
He's more than man-and-woman now.

Touch me – not cold and solid
but finer than air
quicker than light:
how can you understand
whose brains are honeycombed
with sensations,
whose flesh bruises?

Put a bullet through my heart
a bomb in my hand;
I am scatheless as snow unfallen.
Take those flowers home!

Stranger

I'm a stranger to myself
looking down a reversed telescope
at a tiny figure
behind glass of another life
who stands by a sundial
where a tall, fair man is telling time
with one finger,
time that has stopped with the sun
and marguerites staring, yellow-eyed,
and two children playing on the lawn
with a red ball suspended in air.

Haloed in memory's lens
these four are linked
beyond the years' breaking; he
straight, keen as a steeple,
the children unsmudged by shadows,
and she
the stranger I have never met,
only been.

Prisoners

I see you through glass now
cocooned in white
sealed from familiars
receiving flowers and fruit
across barriers.

Cellophane wraps our thoughts;
smiles tied in ribbon –
a nurse with scissors and stop-watch
orders me to go.

Alone with the clock
in the corridor
I'm the one doing time.

Renaissance

I lie still
and the fountain enters me
filling vessels and veins with living water:
the spirit of the fountain
moves over my face.

I am born again
neither man nor woman,
free
from the sad couple
rooted in the grass –
sad because they are two
struggling to be one.

In the Beginning

Before all worlds, alone in the dark,
he called up the sun,
called up the winds and the moon
and waters to spin in his face.

At his word the waters divided
and creatures shaped to his hand –
convolute, curved, spiralled and whorled –
were flung on the sand
with seaweeds belted and scrolled.
Spring tides roared, and rolled in shells
fine as infants' fingernails;
fringed anemones sucking naked rocks
were dark as jellied blood.

In the tiger-lily he saw the tiger;
before the moon
saw men landing in its dust
and gazing down through microscopes
at seventeen thousand invisible tubes
in the lens of a butterfly's eye –
his blueprint for sight.

Creation is imagination
crying in the dark:

Let there be light!

Maker of images
unknown, unseen,
whose need before all needs
is to be loved and known,
holds up a mirror before his face
and breathes into the glass.

I Am

Considering stars,
sand grains, shells –
spiralling infinities –
I am nothing,
uncounted as pebbles,
sparrows, grass,
dispensable as one sperm
in a universe.

Among days, seasons, light-years,
where is my date?
On stone washed over and over
by rivers gone under
centuries' bridges.

And I am all –
universe
unknowable source.
Does not the sun
shine upon me?
A tree gives its shelter
and a lover identity?

Refugees

In the cathedral close
we feel safe
from arguments' ricochet
of bullets in the brain.
Even worker bees drowse
in bell-flowers, and trees
shielded from rebel winds
fold obedient hand over hand.

On clergy lawns there is croquet –
we have been through all the hoops:
answers to unanswerable questions
click into place –
and cucumber sandwiches,
padding for open minds
against truth's bite.

Yet doubt stirs in the wake of bishops
and canons intoning
repentance, absolution –
white-handed washing away our nature.
Armoured in salvation suits
against sinners' pinpricks,
do they, too, feel desire
locked with despair in the body's war
against the spirit?

Violet at Ninety

Descendants stretching beyond her reach –
diminishing pearls on a string –
have long since forgotten her age.
She is pre-history, unreckoned,
head of honeycomb of cells,
some lighted, some shuttered.
When she tells of the Boer War, suffragettes,
horse-trams and buns for a farthing,
they smile indulgent disbelief.

The hungry generations tread on her dreams
knocking on the door in the wrong order.
She sees everything upside down
or in reverse –
clocks cross hands, confusing
minutes with hours as friends drop out
from her shrinking world of musical chairs.

New tides of disorder
wash over her; she remains
a rock in the river unmoved
by the changing climate; an antique fountain
in the city centre.

When a great-great-grandson
old in wisdom, whispers
the secret of happiness in her good ear,
she smiles, suddenly young,
stepping on to uncut grass from her curtained room.

Yew Tree Guest House

In guest-house lounges
elderly ladies shrivel away
wearing bright bangles, beads, jumpers
to colour the waiting day
between breakfast and bed.

Grey widows whose beds and meals are made,
husbands tidied with the emptied cupboards,
live in mortgaged time
disguising inconsequence
with shavings of surface talk, letters
to nieces, stitches dropped in the quick-knit jacket,
picked up for makeweight meaning.

Weekdays are patterned by meals –
sole chance for speculation:
will it be cabbage or peas, boiled fish or fried?
Dead Sunday is dedicated to roast beef –
knives and forks are grips upon existence.
This diversion lengthens the journey;
and since Mrs Porter ceased to come downstairs,
ceased altogether,
the ladies at the Yew Tree Guest House
bend more intently over their soup and sago,
draw closer to the table.

Analyst

Not content with eyes
for the flower, he uses
tweezers, pulling stamens,
stigma, style and ovary,
bruising
the petals apart, searching
what is no longer there.

He has probed too many entries
examining hair, labia
with curious torch
that loses what it lights, provides
inadequate notes.

Somehow he must secrete
communion bread under his tongue
for the microscope.

On Wansfell

I belong nowhere
and to no one
if not to the mountain I lie upon,
the ash tree I lie under
whose leaves' silent music stays
uprising and returning.

Hours, days
are sanded away in the sound
of a harvester –
by this and a leaf-muffled stream,
and the wasp-thin hum of a plane,
are all things bound.

Parting at a Country Station

Your train is late; in time's arrest
we contemplate ragwort, thistles
bristling a bank, unkempt
down-and-outs scratching a living,
signalling colours
of courage and patience.

Reading them we are silent
envying, perhaps, their rootedness
in this wasteland of time.
Winged seeds of words between us
are carried away.

At the platform's edge
one-track travellers
count digital seconds like pulses
with time at their back
unreckoned as wind among foxgloves.

The signal falls; a clock strikes; and they
press forward; we
have taken another line
where no doors slam between us.

Hobson's Choice

Now comes the choice between two fears –
fear of dying and fear of not being dead
when we must go.
Both losses – one of all we know
and one of freedom from it.

Who'd take the course again,
yet who'd stay on it
rolling the same stone up a topless hill,
ever-ever tolling in the brain?

And who'd evaporate
to a hearsay heaven-and-hell –
Eternity
with the same bell reverberating through
light-years of space
and no loved face
to give us back identity
with all we know?

Waiting

Driftwood I have become,
flotsam divided by rocks
between two elements – once
caught in a whirlpool I spun for days
between the dream and its fading.

Now at the world's edge I sit waiting
for the wind to turn –
the grey wind rasping through marram
that has pinned me to sand.
Even the tamarisks have withdrawn
and the sea-holly and evening primrose
that loved the shore.

Sometimes a wisp of hair, sometimes a hand
waving above a wave beckons me on
where I must go to be reborn,
where driftwood knits into flower with maidenhair.

A Very Small Casualty

Flower
lovingly pressed in an album
petals preserved cruciform
colours dried to a moth's wing.

Rabbit
equally flat on tarmac
stamped to a flash of crimson fringed
with skin and hair
parchment-thin under tear and tread.

At human pace I see
spun from the flattened centre
the white scut blown as thistledown
and gleaming jewel-bright, upturned
to the blind indifferent world,
a single eye.

Credo

I believe in Nothing.

And what is Nothing?
The space within you
where God is,
space between friend and friend,
star and star.
Silence of snowfall
and loved ones' absence.

What am I?

A little boat
grappling with angry waves
to keep afloat.
Driven
helpless from shore to shore,
at home only
in the wrench and roar
of waves I defy
that would wrap me in stillness
under storm, under sky
where no winds blow.

I must walk gently
as on a tightrope
now my cup is full,
must balance on air
like a kestrel,
let no drop spill
between dark and dark
as I sing to skylark and sun
lifting up what I hold
to the light.

After Ecclesiastes

The day of death is better than the day of one's birth.

And the end of a party is better than the beginning.
Quietness gathers the voices and laughter
into one cup —
we drink peace.

Crumpled cushions are smoothed as our souls
and silence comes into the room
like a stranger bearing gifts
we had not imagined,
could not have known
without such comings
and such departures.

Unicorn

On the fifth day
the unicorn
must have slipped God's mind
somewhere between horse and goat,
and so was made safe
from man and extinction.
But maybe that
was the primal intention?

Ever seeking a gentle lady
beside whom to lie down,
he travels the world
unguided, invisible.
Archetypal, he faces
the lion beneath the crown.

Beyond this painted emblem
he wanders still,
a shadow seeking the light
in that patient woman who waited
through the dark night of nails
and thorn on the hill.

Words

I
Skimming, bruising, overloading,
diverting the traffic of signs,
words, weighty as stones,
crack the plank across the river
by which I try to reach you.

II
Out of the blue, words
are winged, migratory,
not staying
for answer, passing
overhead,
leaving, perhaps, an edge of song
to be filled in, sounded
through the silent Winter pauses.

III
There are no words for this,
no nets to catch the leap from eye to eye,
no camera to keep
the haloed instant for eternity.

Bolton-Le-Moors, 1960

From Vernon Street in Bolton
you can lift your eyes up to the moors
forgetting traffic, grimed infirmary
and the Blind School where they weave baskets
in compensation.
Between mills' open fingers
you can see them
tawny as sleeping mastiffs
stretched out in the sun.
And Breightmet, rashed with bungalows,
is magical in mist
that kindly scarves a see-through school
with evening amethyst.
Never before in industry's complex
have I felt heather
and wind in the grasses –
the wild and the worked-on working together,
spinning the music of mills
from earth's resources.

The Betterware Man

The Betterware man
stands at the back door and knocks
but I will not let him in.
On the doorstep he opens his case, displays
brushes, stain-removers, pan-scrubs
to scour my soul – my soul is scoured
by that gentle voice:
'This cleans cleaner than clean, removes
stains from inside the cup'.

I never feel dingier
than when I say 'No'
to the Betterware man –
his goods are so good,
better than best,
lasting longer than life.

He's no right to pester me
with persuasion, promises, free gifts –
today a needle-threader
till I'm drawn through myself –
but most of all pity
that plugs me with guilt.
He pleads as with a daughter,
and I shut the door in his face.

Now he's gone I'm all wrung out
like a dish-cloth of not-clean water.

The Mill Clock

The day he brought that old clock from the mill
and nailed it to the wall
he nailed his life there.
Morning and evening checked its time, Sundays
climbed on a chair to wind it,
set the pendulum
tick-tocking with his heartbeat.

On holidays he fretted, couldn't sleep
for listening to its silence,
came home early to wind it –
set it by the radio,
tilted it one degree as a careful mother
adjusts a pram to the wind,
folded a newspaper like a nappy
to stuff behind.
Sometimes it would go for half-an-hour;
once it ticked all day –
that night he slept like a child.
Next morning, silence.

After they took the clock away
he sat alone
jingling its rusty nails as he gazed
at the white space, the face of death
on the wall
ever with him, pacing round the house
losing things, forgetting things, but mostly
forgetting the time.

Love's Advocate

I remember sitting together in parks
leaning over bridges
counting trout and swans
holding hands under arches
kissing away suns
and moons into darkness.

I remember platform good-byes
last-minute trains
slamming us apart
and my non-self walking back alone.
I remember smaller things:
a pebble in my shoe
and you throwing a match-box on the Serpentine.

I stood still hearing the years
flow over and over
as over a stone
in a river-bed
polishing, cleaning, wearing away.
But I still remember the last day.

What I cannot remember is how I felt –
mind, love's advocate,
must remind heart
of the end, the abyss.
The bottom of the world remains;
each day climbs to a new start.

Loneliness Is a Lyric Poem

Loneliness is alone on a canal path
saluting a passing barge
for someone to wave back.

Is walking a station platform
waiting for the next train –
even unhopeful hope
is better than none.

Is on a seat in the park;
maybe someone will come
and talk and tear it away,
ease the going home
where is no home.

Loneliness is a lyric poem
spurned by the *avant-garde* – a theme
ancient, enduring as love and death.

Clown

He was safe
behind the whitened face
and red nose of his trade,
vocation more certain
than doctor's or priest's
to cheer and heal.

Hidden away from himself
he could always make us laugh
turning troubles like jackets
inside out, wearing
our rents and patches.

Tripping up in trousers too long
he made us feel tall;
and when we watched him
cutting himself down,
missing the ball,
we knew we could cope.

What we never knew
was the tightrope he walked
when the laughter had died.
Nowhere to hide in the empty night,
no one to catch his fall.

Paint Box

He tried to tell them what he felt,
could say it only in colours –
Sunday's white page shading to grey
of evening clocks and bells-in-the-rain.
Monday morning, bright yellow brass
of a cock crowing.
Story-time, purple.
Scarlet is shouting in the playground.

His world's a cocoon
round as an egg, an acorn
sprouting green.
The schoolroom square and hard;
his desk hard and square
facing the enemy blackboard.

'You must learn to read,' they said
and gave him a painting-book alphabet.
Apple swelled beautifully red. Balloon
expanded in blue.
C was a cage for a bird;
his brush wavered through
painting himself
a small brown smudge inside.

Boy with Kite

I am master of my kite, and
the wind tugs against me
on blue ropes of air.
Above tasselled trees
my kite glides and swoops,
pink-and-yellow falcon surging loose
from my tight fist.

White string bites
into flesh; my wrist
flexes like a falconer's.

I am dancing with my kite
heel-and-toe to earth,
body braced
against the fleet north-easter laced
with fraying clouds.

Lifted steeple-clear
of church and school and hill
I am master of my world.

Limbo

Flung with door-slam and whistle-blow
into this carriage
I'm a snapshot torn
between two faces,
torn through myself
who yesterday in the garden
weeded and tended, mother among flowers,
asking only the quiet house,
long evening silences, and slow
peace of sunsets.

Now I'm in strange country –
fields, farms, steeples hurtle by
relentless in rhythm.
A woman talks to my incompleteness.
Is she, too, driven
by this terrible engine?
Rhythm, rhythm, railway, river
running voice accompaniment
to emptiness.
Sky and self all hollow.
I am outside, locked out from return.
No house will open to a wanderer
who's lost the key.

Understudy

She's a trained low-profile lady
obeying the signs –
Keep out, Keep off the grass –
keeping her place backstage
until her call
from the undressing-room. All
her performances submerged
in her major-minor role
of understudy.

Reply to a Philistine

Not even if you went on hands and knees,
read all the books,
put yourself through hoops,
could you enter this dimension.
Your sight is down the barrel of a gun.

It's not a matter of getting there,
of endeavour and desire,
but of knowing the unmapped country.

To see this you bring field-glasses
and a compass.
There's no
microscope can show you
that primrose by the river's brim
as something more.

A Child's Guide to Philosophy

Things as they are
are as they are because
they aren't
otherwise, said Kant.

Before him Aristotle,
thinking about thinking,
drew a cork from a bottle
to find the world altered by drinking.

Descartes thought
and said *Sum*.
Hobbes found life nasty
and short.

Schopenhauer would rather
have never been born –
it was he should have poured
the hemlock and drunk it.
But Kierkegaard,
though crippled, deplored
lack of faith for the leap
in the dark –
he himself wouldn't funk it.

Bentham found goodness in pleasure;
Mill disagreed.
How can we draw up a creed
with such contradictions
in efforts to know what cannot be known?
From Wittgenstein's answer –
'Get rid of the question'?

Scapegoat

The ancients – all males, of course –
wrote the story in reverse.
The Tale of the Rib,
woven from pride and guilt,
is irrelevant.
It all began with Eve
lying alone in the grass
enjoying the apple
he hadn't the wit to discover.
Politely she handed it
to him who bit it greedily
undoing her
with his lost innocence.

Adam, the betrayer,
hearing his name
pouring down in accusation,
put up his umbrella
covering himself,
leaving Eve in the rain.

Emily Dickinson

Others wore colours; I wore white
for one who never came –
whose coming was his going that
left me here alone.
I'll not expect a knocking on
my name carved in stone.

The Party

The best party of all is when,
The host being absent, the guests –
relations, friends, and neighbours – gather
to drink his health now he's taken
the final cure.

Praises sung, they relapse
into themselves, rejoicing
in this bringing together
by one whose going resolves
frictions in the estranged,
the half-remembered, half-forgotten,
all changed,
who wish him the happiest birthday
with no returns.

Autumn at Whitewell

I stand upon dry leaves;
others come spinning down
while trodden memories
rustle through my brain
vague as river sound
lulling the afternoon.

Now prickling rain
scratches through sense to thought:
I see why Autumn fills
more than woods and roads
with lifetime flower and fall
pressing the colours close,
packing promise lost and tall
in smallest range.

Strange that experience
grown out of hand and brain
should drop back leaf by leaf
each vein
a scrawled reminder . . .
A robin threads his song between
needles of larch and rain.

Roots

Even a tree has inclination
leaning
to east or west,
north or south
which we, sophisticated
with layer minds, prejudices,
preconceptions,
would label left and right,
rich and poor, unseeing
through the impartial swing of the wind
in the seed's setting,
the root and branch propulsion
of a tree's integrity.

We, who grow through choices
regarding the tree
as swayed beyond itself,
passive, obedient to changing winds,
commanding voices,
have lost direction in the breakaway
of mind
to power beyond capacity to hold
from roots that bind.

Sun Up

Apollo, Christ and God, all three
met in the first sunrise.
God's hand before Apollo's eyes
shadowed the land with the first tree,
and the man behind the sun came down
and walked upon the sea.

'We are the Light of the World,' said Christ
and Apollo in unison –
fire and flesh of the hidden spark.
'And I,' said God, 'am the Three-in-One
who struck the match in the dark.'

Partridge

She was round and warm and brown,
homely and soft as a fresh cob loaf.
She nestled you to comfort
from stings of nettles, thistles,
and wasp-thin tongues.
One could feel her
feathering her eggs, folding them
under her breast,
shuffling her wings
till all were safely gathered.

Her warmth of welcome shone
across a field;
you came to her out of the rain;
the wind lay down when she was near.
Sorrow that dropped from you
was dried, and laughter shook
easily as ears of corn.

I never heard her sing;
her song was herself.

Orpheus in the Underground

In the moment of looking back
From the top step
Of the escalator
The white flower of her face
Tilted towards him
Melted into the crowd.
And the tunnel sucked her underground.

The crowd surged upward
Pushing him into
The concrete world,
Mirrors mocked him; voices
Demanded rock for dancing;
Stamping feet stamped on
The hems of grief; breaking
His guitar strings; hands
Unstrung him, flung him
Singing into the Thames.

Protean Lover

I have a lover, but he's made of paper;
I read him back through words unwritten, find
A stranger hidden in the space between
Lines that lead me dancing, leave me blind.

I have a lover, but he's made of glass;
I see straight through him till I only see
My searching eyes reflected and reflecting
Receding images of him in me.

I have a lover, but he's made of water;
Lost to myself I plunge and swim alone
Away from the crumbling shore, compelled by the current
To drink the life I seek until I drown.

Starlings

Starlings have good ears:
they pick up threads of song
from blackbirds, thrushes to deceive us
with variations from chimney-pots.

Starlings fool us
with originality,
cuckooing the lover
with Spring rhapsodies,
luring schoolboys out of school.

Starlings are found in libraries,
pecking among bookshops,
nesting a season in museums.
Adept at worming in dictionaries,
darting through leaves
of encyclopaedias, this breed,
crop-full of knowledge,
is practised in the art
of eclectic harvesting
whose corn serves to gloss
their borrowed plumes.

The Shaping Spirit

As a woman selecting threads
From a swatch of colours,
He selects words
Of many shades, tones, nuances.
Each to be weighed, measured,
Tongue-tested, and applied
According to relevance, shaped
Into stanzas, and what then
But a conglomerate
Of words unfired as a lump of clay
Without the shaping spirit?
Not to be teased into life
By will or desire,
But by giving air and space
To that which, seasoned as wood,
Catches fire.

No Reply at Christmas

I have called you many times;
it's always No Reply.
And the answer from Enquiries
is my own question –
'What town and name?'
when the name's not in the book.

In the dark I go out, walking
through the Christmas wood
where the star that stood over a stable
is under a cloud.

When I ask its position
in the heavens, they laugh deriding
faith in an old story
woven of myth and fairy-tale,
and leave me in the cold
wind blowing away even rags
of comfort.

But I cannot go back –
my footprints are filled with snow,
the track obliterated.
And I cannot go on through the blind
night. I will forget time and the Winter,
and wait, not seeing
but hoping.

Return

I was always away from myself,
a shadow opening
doors without rooms, falling
short of being,
nobody's ghost, seeing
unseen,
a stranger meeting
me face to face in the dark.

Now all of the rooms and beds are mine;
I am mistress of the switches.
Darkness rocks me, day
breaks into poetry and music.
No one locks me out of the inner room.

If the house feels empty
I think of those
whose absence has made me someone
I could never have known.

Vision

Here at the gate where understanding ends
Vision begins, for only silence calls
Louder than any voice, and darkness bends
My stubborn will to truth.
I cannot see the way and yet I pass
Beyond the measured boundaries of mind.
Shine on me as the sun on window-glass
Till I transmit the light I cannot find.

Edward Thomas

Out of the woods he came;
From some green world his other life began
In way-back bondage to a god half man,
Half goat who knew each bird and leaf by name.

Often the stars he wondered at went blind
As he unseeing struggled in the dark,
Brick-walled captive of a searching mind,
Lost to his loved ones, trampling the spark
He lived by in the mud.

Through this quick anger poisoning the blood
There comes a bead of song, a thread of sound
Lifting the choking gloom; he wakes to see
The first primrose, a wood anemone
Whiter than milk from Winter underground.

And the world is light, light as the first day;
Creation holds him singing in its power,
Perceiving truth in beauty hidden away
In a wren's egg, rain, and dust on a nettle flower.

Master Cotton Spinner

Bolton, Lancashire, in the 1950s

The mill's black finger
Thrusting higher through the mist
Than the steeple of St. Peter,
Has pointed his childhood to work,
Money, and power at the top,
Shadowed each working hour,
Bricked-in his dreams,
Written his will in a smoke-plume.

Overalled at seventeen,
He trod his father's mill barefoot
On hot, greased boards,
Serving the mules,
Nursing the thread
Into white cocoons, fattened
Upon whirling spindles
In damp heat tasting of oil,
Noise dimming speech to lip-language
As he learned the cool feel
Of cotton ripened by Egyptian sun.

Grading each load, was himself upgraded
To foreman, manager; he remained
Servant of machines, friend of spinners,
Bob, Jim, and Fred in the warm club
Fumed with beer and tobacco,
Refuge and home where differences were levelled
On the same floor.

He played bowls for Hawkshaw's,
Visited them in hospital –
Spinners' cancer fruiting in their vitals
Was reckoned a voluntary, while he
Sat uneasy in his office chair.

Red sky at morning: the spinners' warning;
The rising sun, crimson,
Soundless, sounded a gong
With cheap, bright frocks from Japan,
Gaudy towels from Pakistan
To dazzle in chain-stores.

It was short time for them.
The mill closed one day a week,
And then two.
Idle machines rusted, were scrapped.
His new job was scrapping the older men.
Evenings found him empty, threadbare,
A blind drawn down his face.

Still the colourful bales flowed in
Easy as eastern flowers, cajoling
Buyers to ignore snags in the cloth.

Through silence of spindles and looms,
Queues at the labour exchange,
And rents unpaid, still the flood,
Ominous as the Styx,
Gulped and rose outside the gates.

Seven hours
Round a boardroom table reduced it
To a trickle in the Take Over.
Hawkshaw's brick-built name written
Over a century's endeavour,
Survived on paper – in small print.

New managers were enlisted,
Young men roped against disaster
In competition's tug-of-war.
The last of the old comrades –
Deadwood Jim and Fred, were his for the cutting.

He was a job for the chairman
Who shook his hand, presenting him
With a gold watch and chain.
Unmanned, redundant, unnamed in the crowd,
He watched Hawkshaw's chimney felled like a tree.
But a tree falls whole, stretched proud to its highest leaf;
The doomed chimney collapsed like a toy
Into smoking rubble;
You could hear a sparrow fall
In brick-dust of that choking silence.

He returns daily to tread the mill
In the supermarket risen in its stead,
Fingering tins as he fingered the spindles,
Pulling the years' thread from his ravelled sleeve.

Imprint

It is a footprint
In sand or snow
With nobody there.

It is a voice.
But when I question, I hear
Only the wind
Fingering dead oak leaves,
Lifting
The stiffened fir tree branches.

It is the form
Of a hare – grasses
Still warm
And rounded from its resting,
But empty as air.

It is nothing and no one
Who can be known,
Only the imprint
Of somebody there.

All Hallows

(for Hilbre)

Walking among the antlered oaks,
Beeches, birches going gold,
Bracken, fox and squirrel-red,
I walk with ghosts.

It's not the sorrow of being old
But simple grief to be the last
Which overlays these coloured joys
With none to share the memoried past
Time only half destroys.

I wait until the ripe sun sets
And watch the trees,
How they count the days with leaves
And no regrets.

Sundowner

In the last light of a late
October day
Let me go like a flake
Of whitening ash as I slowly burn
Down from the sun towards the day's return.

Being

Animals do not cling;
They stand
Patient in fields, not waiting.
Unfooled by hope,
Unringed by promises,
Being, not understood
But felt, is all,
Lived breath by breath
In the deep, dark wood of unknowing
Where death, their birthright,
Is not wrapped in words and flowers.

Olympia

The smooth indifferent moon looked down
On her double, unwrinkled in Alpheus – sacred river
Sounding through Coleridge's broken dream.
For us it girdled Olympia
With memories, rumours
Of discus-throwers through lost centuries.

We'd restored the crumbling pillars with echoes,
Triumphs and disasters; stood
Wordless before the flying feet
Of Hermes immortalized, stone-bound, his face
By magic of Praxiteles
Printed on the future.

Statues, shrines, the empty stadium grassed
From sweat of running feet;
Thunderous Zeus's temple risen from rock –
These recalled as we stood in the moonlit garden
That held its breath with leaves,
Listening
For distant tramping, spears clashing on shields,
Hearing only the wind in the white petals
Of roses caught in the iron balustrade.
Till a single nightingale
Aroused the charm to sing the heroes back
From hills of legend and forgotten graves.

Perennial Love Song

I to you am a shadow
slanting, sometimes, across the page,
in-and-out through chinks unguarded,
present only in secluded corners
when the garden is quiet, the room empty,
echoing round the walls
with words a backward glance recalls.

But you to me are the sun
breaking through protective trivia,
catching me out
in gaps of thought, and when at nights
I try to bury you in books,
a beanstalk sets the green, compulsive ladder
to unimagined heights.

Shutting Out the Sun

For days he has sat in the dark room
Developing ideas, consulting
References, and drawing
Conclusions unfixed on the film.
Baffled, he tries another take,
Dares not let in the sun –
That would expose another kind of failure.

Running to waste, energy
Spins the weathercock all ways
Sending him about, but not out
Of himself.
Which way he goes he returns
To a blind corner
In the dark room.
Which way he stands
He stands in his own light.

Prophet

In purple and gold
he towers above them gathered
to hear his word illuminating
the mystery
absorbed centuries before, imploring
a lead into depths beyond understanding.
But his tongue is a blade
cutting away their ground, upturning
grass they've walked over unquestioning.

With upraised arm
he shows them the keys
and locks them out of the garden.

He lays a pavement before them, crushing
half-opened flowers,
and directs them to shelves of science
and philosophy.
And they come away hearing
the gate closing against them
a second time.

A Poem Is a Painting

A poem is a painting that is not seen;
A painting is a poem that is not heard.

That's what poetry is —
a painting in the mind.
Without palette and brush
it mixes words into images.
The mind's edge sharpens the knife
slashing the canvas with savage rocks,
twisting trees and limbs into tortuous shapes
as Van Gogh did,
or bewitched by movement's grace,
captures the opalescent skirts
of Degas' ballet dancers.

But words on the page
as paint on canvas
are fixed.
It's in the space between
the poem is quickened.

Naked Ostrich

People meeting at parties
or tête-à-tête across desk or table,
are of the same species –
the naked ostrich.
Talk of politics, the arts, the weather,
we're in daylight country,
mention death, and a blind comes down:
they shrink and silence grows.
Switch to gardens, wildlife, travel,
and we're above ground again.

I find myself alone;
no coat in the wind –
the subject can be changed, but not the wind.
'Why must you ask,' they say,
'what cannot be answered?'
They are wise;
contentment lies deep, unstirred.
Out in the wind are no replies,
only echoes of Pilate's question.

Changing Colour

It happened slowly
as a cygnet turns from grey to white,
but in Saville Street it happened in reverse –
from white to ivory to café-au-lait
to strong black coffee,
and from drab to bright –
greys and duns to ruby, turquoise, emerald,
from brass to reed –
reed music quickening soft, sandalled feet
hushing the tapping pavements
in rhythm of a dance,
strange tongues and voices at front doors
confusing us.

Now we've learned the tune
in bangles, saris, turbans,
flashing jewels
from molten sand and stone –
hot jungle music
vibrating through the northern rain.

Comparison with a Sunflower

Seeded, brown beyond admiration,
The sunflower, having passed its prime,
Expects no responses from the sun.
I, too, like the sunflower,
Demanding nothing, am liberated,
Free from erratic seasons of the heart,
Am suspended, wingless, between
Pendulum swings tick-tocking away
The emptiness of age when, for me,
Unlike the sunflower, mindless on its stalk,
Awareness sharpens with the shortening days.

So Little It Can Take

One leaf on a line
cannot delay a train,
but many fallen together
heaped, and damped by rain
can halt the screaming express,
disrupt appointments, prevent
meetings and bonds of love.
A sideways move can shake
dice from a ladder's foot
to the head of a snake.
So little it can take
to change design to disorder,
man into bone
as, with time, a drop of water
can change the face of a stone.

After Verlaine

It snows in my soul
As it snows on the ground
And the cold in my soul
Is the cold in the sound
Of a snow-laden wind
From a maiden-white cloud.

Very fine are the flakes
Very soft is the fall
Mother-soft fingers
Are weaving a shawl,
Are folding a shawl
Until the thread breaks.

Walking Back

Walking again along those well-loved paths
misted with bluebells,
between translucent beeches, young in leaf,
and strong horse-chestnuts
holding up white candles to the day,
is a kind of bereavement.

Family and friends departed,
and many dead,
every cottage altered by new owners,
and the white house where we lived
painted, smartened, tastefully modernised.
It was a Georgian rectory where
Jane Austen might have lived –
a little shabby, threadbare,
yet breathing history, a home for poets
more than novelists, it was
a Walter-de-la-Marish sort of house.
Shadowed branches in the moonlight
laced the walls mysteriously.
Often an owl called from the poplar tree
slim as a mast, the tree where one star,
like a bird, lodged in the topmost branches.

I used to stand against the garden wall
looking up to the house I loved and vowed
never to leave.
The marguerites in front were little moons
silver, silent, in the mothy night.
Now all is changed – the younger son went first,
and then the father. All the rest have followed.
One by one they went, but I must stay
returning sometimes, foolishly, to recall
memories better left
sleeping among the fells, under the trees,
and withering with these bluebells. Strange
how one can bury all but these!

The Gymnasts

All at once I saw them
whirling arms and legs – the gymnasts
doing handstands on the high fell
linking past and future.
Here are the four winds caught
bridled and harnessed to our use.
Could Caratacos in his wild rides
have seen them! Now it seems
plans from another planet in our hands
are witnessed on Cold Clough Moor.
Tall and slim and white
twirling the air, they offer warmth and light
to thirty thousand living there below
in the rugged valley feathered with rowan and birch.
For them, no power-cuts or strikes
only the wind's variations.
But my first sight of the twenty-four
racing, while rooted, in unison
was wonder and delight electrified.

From Walden

Thoreau's house in the woods.

'Three chairs –
one for solitude, two for company –
three for society,'
a bed, a table, what more
for a wish?
Or for warmth, a wood fire?

Worlds of Spring and Summer
stream through my windows.
Time and space for thought: I dwell
without stairs on many levels,
fired by unanswered questions –
how comes the clam, thick-shelled
sunk deep in river mud
by its rainbow colours?
Or the celandine its shine
even without the sun?

I have east and west in my windows;
the door opens south
inviting me out, shutting me
against rain.
I need no ornaments, having all outside.
I sit among grasses
that gather no dust, am rich
with earth's coinage
that spills and is ever replenished.

Which way I go in the woods
I follow the Indian's track:
first come, he is wise
reading the wind, and the moon's seasons.
By the moon, not the sun,
his days are measured,
and by winters his life.

Lights, dazzling-bright,
he leaves to the white man

whose power will eat away forests
and flatten the earth.
Everywhere
the white man set his foot
the land is sore.
While the Indian inhabits Nature,
the white man invades.
In darkness and silence
the Indian finds his way
through brushwood and pine,
even the blue jay
is quiet at his coming; the owl
salutes him.

Thoreau Speaks from Walden

Sitting alone in my cabin
watching the woodchucks play
and the striped racoons
streaking through the shadows,
I know I have much to learn from the Indian
who is free
while the minister confines himself
in words and argument.

Civilized man will rule the world
outside himself, forgetting
what the Indian has not lost
and both were given,
for both have been children.

Civilization!
What have you done that so many
live lives of quiet desperation?
I'll return to my three chairs
with Alcott and Emerson;
we'll talk the night into sunrise
till we find there's a way through the forest
without destroying the trees.

Days

Days, like sand, run through the hour-glass,
Flash by on the ticker-tape,
Turn the Summer into Winter,
Change the shape
Of facts and faces, rub out names
Cut with passion into tree-trunks,
Type out other ones instead,
Moss-fingered, fill the letters written
In stone to tell us who is dead,
Unweave the plover's nest in passing –
Days are egg-shells where I tread.

Defeathered

Unlocking the bathroom;
handing over the keys of the house;
exposing privacies
while hiding the soul, invaded
by helpers, yet needing their help,
resenting
the necessity of pity;
accepting, receiving, thanking
without giving, being
on the wrong side of the door, pretending
to be happy, free from pain while knowing
the peacock's treasured tail
defeathered,
is to act out 'the last stage of all'
as though
the curtain were not about to fall.

From the Day Room

The people here are not here.
Where are they gone who have left themselves behind?
Why does this one pluck her skirt all day?
And why, this Monday morning,
does the grey man, stuffed in a wheelchair,
not read the *Sunday Times*
propped up before him?

From the day room a lake
glitters before us; snowdrops
whiten and shake in the grass, and squirrels
raise question-mark tails,
aptly inverted for questions
that cannot be answered.

Perhaps I
am saddest of all who feel the Spring
groping around us, and the call
in the air inviting us on
into the sun and a world
of rising sap and renewal.

The Leave Train

The rain is moving;
Out of the window I am waving;
Sister, daughter, friend, and son
Wait on the platform unaware
The train has gone.

Behind them, relations, people
At parties, in shops, in the street –
People I know by sight but not to meet:
They cannot see
The light gone green for me
On a line untravelled.
One day they, one at a time,
Will take the train,
Each to a different destination
Not yet printed in the guide.
Yet every ticket's ordered in advance.

Under the clock they hurry
Home and back again
Making a dance of the time-table, believing
The train they must catch
Is not yet running.

Noah Changes His Venue

The animals went in two by two
and came out one by one.
But many things happened between –
they quarrelled and killed in the dark
for food and a place in the sun,
but there ain't no sun in the ark.

Meeting and spawning they ran out of air,
and drank the ocean dry,
and all for lack of elbow room,
planned to conquer the sky.

Now see where we are
perched on a star,
and Noah is standing by.

In Reverse

And man created God
in his own image.
Examining the puppet in his hands,
he saw that it was not
very good.

'But now that we are here,' he said,
'We must try to make the world,
which you began,
a better place.

You, who lighted the sun,
flung moon and stars into space,
spread out the sea, earth, and all there is,
felt lonely out there
and produced us for conversation,
which became a monologue
condensed into a question.

Now we've drained the earth,
polluted the air and water
for our convenience and comfort,
reclaiming all you gave
to turn into waste,
is there an end?'

Probing the planets
and the power in a microbe,
the question searches the universe.
Because the answer is silence
we fill it with noise.

The Terrible Beauty of Efficiency

Rivington Village post office
as I knew it sixty years ago
with its scratched wooden table, ink-well,
cross-nibbed pen and blotting-paper reflecting
bucolic signatures,
its packets of Woodbines
and jars of spiralling barley-sugar,
is all *changed, changed utterly:*
A terrible beauty is born.

There's a counter smooth with efficiency
and a shining metal grille
guarding the new, smart postmistress
(since the old one was mugged) –
Oh, so smart you'd never hear her say
like the other,
after giving me the wrong stamp
(which I told her I'd licked),
'Never mind,' as she took it back,
'It'll dry!'

Olivia (Aged Nearly Five)

You'd think she'd stepped from a Greek myth,
Oenone, perhaps,
running naked on the grass,
her long copper hair, with a pink rose,
floating as she moved.
Too young to mourn for Paris,
or be touched by sorrow, innocence
unassailed,
one with the trees, and the flowers
snatched as she passed.
Without words, holding our breath,
cupping our hands,
we watched movement and dance untaught:
the instant was too brimmed to hold.

Lament of a Twentieth Century Poet

I am that unfortunate thing, a lyric poet.
It's *verboten* to sing; I must plan
my verse as an architect can, transpose
and prune every phrase till nobody knows
what I'm trying to say, go to bed
with Thesaurus, and welcome the day
with the O. E. D. 'You should spend
each week-end at a Workshop for Poems.
They'll hammer your lyrics, and nail
them to meanings you can't understand.'

Oh, hard
to cut out the tongue of a natural bard
and leave it all to the brain!

'Happiness Writes White'

Philip Larkin

When I'm happy
I despise writing,
and live.
I wander through woods and fields,
and plunge in the sea
exultant, free.

When I'm happy
I despise those
bent over books in libraries,
breathing the thin paper air
of bookshops, directed
by print's authority.

But when I'm unhappy
I'm driven
to sit down and write
with no more direction
than a weathercock
in changing winds.

Retired

With russet apples and vintage claret,
as prickly Spring through Summer into Autumn,
she mellows.
Acid in her tongue drops from her lips
sweet as the juice of a ripened plum
till hearers, once children bitten and stung,
believe themselves deceived:
desks, sharp-lidded, seats
of apprehension, hardened in memory,
soften to duck-down, cushioned as her breasts.

Like Aphrodite, tired of jealous gods,
she rinses herself of foam,
steps down from the platform, finds her home
on common ground.

Suddenly It's Winter

Suddenly it's Winter where I stand,
a bare, wind-twisted tree –
you can see I've been pulled many ways –
my hair, now grey, reproaches me
for so much fallen
like leaves dry-curled
as paper in a bin,
and bronze chrysanthemums,
a row of wrung-out mops.

Let others come
thumb-sucking into the world
to review holes in the road,
cul-de-sacs, wrong turnings
and signposts showing
all that might have been different.

Whichever way we choose
the curse we are born with
tracks and attacks us
in the fights we sometimes win
and the battle we must lose.

Jeu d'Esprit

Longfellow and Tennyson,
Laureates of their time,
Pearly Kings of Poetry
Buttoned up in rhyme.

But years, the *great black oxen*,
Have trodden underfoot
Each royal reputation,
Destroyed it at the root.

When Auden re-read Tennyson
Scales fell from his eyes:
He saw through critics' blindness
The fashionable lies.

And Longfellow in Boston,
Once loved, revered, and famed,
Has vanished from anthologies;
You seldom hear him named.

I remembered Hiawatha
And the schoolroom's loud refrain:
By the shores of Gitche Gumee . . .
So I read it once again.

Dark before me rose the forest,
Rose the Moon above her daughter,
Nokomis, nursing Hiawatha,
Standing with her feet in water.

On I read till night was ended
With the dawn call of the owlet;
Weary was I; trochees running,
Set to automatic pilot.

Loss of Grief

How strangely unfulfilled I am
Since grief has lost its power
To sting and hold me captive
Through every wasted hour.

Intensity is slackened
As feeling drains away:
I can watch the sunset weaken
And the moon rise into day
Till the commonplace absorbs me
In its rhythm; I become
An ordinary person
Whose inner voice is dumb –

I long to be the poet I am
But the words will never come.

A Box of Silver Birch

Give me a box of silver birch,
something light and easily burnt,
but don't enclose me
airless in earth; I belong to the moors
the miles of bracken and heather.
I've been a prisoner long enough
now let me be wherever
the changing wind blows me.

PART TWO

POEMS FOR YOUNGER READERS

Sweet Music Is Not Only Drawn from Lute

Sweet music is not only drawn from lute
Or fashions wrought from man's own brain,
There's music in the steady fall of rain.
The blackbird's voice in itself is a flute
So full and clear that listening man is mute.
What sound is sweeter than the lark's refrain,
Than golden fields of ever-whisp'ring grain,
Or hymn for which there is no substitute?

And in the city are sweet sounds forgot?
From factory roof who hears the pigeons' call?
For some 'tis drowned by traffic like as not:
There's rhythm in the horse's trot withal,
And from the tall clock tower who has forgot
The merry chimes of bells as eve doth fall?

Cheltenham Ladies' College Poetry prize 1925.

Who and Why?

Who made the grass and the five pointed stars
And the moon that lies white on my nursery bars?
Why does the wind blow and who gave the wings
To butterflies, birds and hundreds of things
That fly in the Summer time over my head,
That tap on the windowpane when I am in bed?

Why is the Winter so cold and so white
With such little playtime and such a long night?
Who put the yellow and green in the Spring
And planted the crocuses round in a ring
As bright as a circus and red tulips tall
And upright as soldiers that march by the wall?

Who put such buckets and buckets of sand
Along by the sea at the edge of the land?
If I took out my spade and I started to do
Hard digging from now till I'm seventy-two,
There still would be buckets and bucketsful there
For other small children with gold in their hair.

Do you think I will ever be seventy-two?
I hope so, for I have so much to do
With aeroplanes, tigers and castles and kings –
But who is the person who made all these things?
The answer you give me is always the same
So God must be wonderful, then if I came
From God as you say, I am wonderful too –
I am glad because there is so much to do.

Hitting the Moon

I'm Rodney on my red-hot motorbike
roaring between hedges,
ripping the air like calico,
rattling angrier bullets
than machine guns as I go.

My armour against the world
is shiny black and white plastic.
Zipped inside my black jacket
no one can reach me;
under my white helmet
I'm not afraid any more.
The speed needle flicks to ninety;
curves race round me
hugging my flight
from narrow streets, hindering traffic,
restrictions, family rows.

On my pulsing hot-blood motorbike
I'm Rodney new-made –
more than a boy, more
than a man.
Unafraid of the world I conquer –
lashing out the miles, leaning
on the wind, learning
how it feels to be hitting the moon.

The River Idle

Here the River Idle sidles leisurely across the plain
Broad between the bending willows, grey beneath the tilting rain.
Like a looking glass reflecting silent trees and whistling train.

Toyshop train that rattles seaward, over bridges clattering on
Sometimes by the river, sometimes fields away in miles alone,
Never stopping, never slowing till the clockwork journey's done.

Under bridges running darkly, running on yet not away,
The Idle winds unsleeping Ss through the seasons, green and grey,
Where endings run into beginnings in the round of night and day.

Kingfisher

Brown as nettle-beer, the stream
Shadow freckled, specked with sun,
Slides between the trees.

Not a ripple breaks in foam;
Only the frilled hedge-parsley falls
White upon the ground.
No insect drills the air; no sound
Rustles among the reeds.
Bird and leaf and thought are still
When shot from the blue, a kingfisher
Flashes between the ferns –
Jewelled torpedo sparkling by
Under the bridge and gone –
Yet bright as a bead behind the eye,
The image blazes on.

Dead Blackbird

The blackbird used to come each day
listening, head-sideways, for movement under the lawn,
stabbing his yellow crocus bill
precisely in,
pulling out a pink elastic worm.

In Winter with flirted tail
he landed on the sill for crumbs
ousting sparrows, blue-tits, even robins.
Soot black, sleek,
his plumage shone like a dark man's head.

But this morning I looked out of the window
and saw him dead –
a crumpled bunch of feathers,
rocking in the wind.

I have never seen anything dead
except flies
and stuffed animals in museums
where they make them look alive.
Dead people are hidden away,
tidied into boxes,
covered with flowers.
The living talk about the dead in low voices.
Is death so ugly, so uncomfortable
that people are afraid?

I am much more afraid of what I cannot see.
But I can see the blackbird;
and I know these crumpled feathers
are only rags of him, not he
with his crocus-yellow bill.

Man Alive

Tigers velvet-striped with cunning,
Muscles rippling to attack;
Midnight braziers burning, turning
Light to darkness, red to black.

Tigers gripped with savage mating,
Tensed in combat's leashed up breath.
Snarling shadows; splintered sunlight,
Life resurgent over death.

Tigers locked in living, dying;
Leafing trees made food for earth;
White birds into sunset flying;
Death translated into birth.

The First Day of Spring

There's strength in the sun, strength in the wind;
Burn hot, blow cold is the strength behind
The bud that breaks through Winter's rind.

Follow the white root stretched below
Mysteries of sleep and snow
Further than measure and mind can go.

Out of the dark, made strong through cold,
Limbs are stirring; leaves unfold;
Crocus fingers tipped with gold
Point to the light that brims and spills
Into the cities, over the hills
Till the world with warmth and movement fills.

Heatwave

Heat all over; not a lark can rise
Into the arching sun;
The moor like a lion sleeping lies –
Rough mane on burning stone.
Not a harebell shakes; the wild blue flags
Of wind are folded up.
Here on the hill the air is still
As water in a cup.

Fall

October dew glitters
on morning's eyelashes,
swells and slides down stem
to breathing earth
wreathed in convolvulus,
warm, maternal earth
involved with birth not death.
Traveller's joy is seed
riding the wind
where trumpets outblow the season
misting brassy lips
with fiery breath.
And slow, cold fingers wait unclasped
round the root beneath.

Sally

She was a dog-rose kind of girl;
elusive, scattery as petals;
scratchy sometimes, tripping you like briars.
She teased the boys
twisting this way and that, not to be tamed
or taught any more than the wind.
Even in school the word 'ought'
had no meaning for Sally.
On dull days
she'd sit quiet as a mole at her desk
delving in thought.
But when the sun called
she was gone, running the blue day down
till the warm hedgerows prickled the dusk
and moths flickered out.

Her mother scolded; Dad
gave her the hazel-switch,
and her head was stuffed with feathers
and a starling tongue.
But they couldn't take the shine out of her.
Even when it rained
You felt the sun saved under her skin.
She'd a way of escape
Laughing at you from the bright end of a tunnel,
Leaving you in the dark.

Ward F4

There is no weather in my room,
a white cube, bare
except for a bedside chest; one chair.
The window behind my bed
looks blind on a blind wall,
but I cannot turn my head.

No sky; no sun;
one lamp with hard green shade
is my daylight
and nightlight.
(No flowers, please, nowhere
to put them but on the floor.)
I face the brown door, stare
at the black knob, waiting . . . .

Nurses come and go
brisk, kind under crackling starch.
They give me pills, injections
with cheerful remarks about the weather.
But there is no weather in my room.

Autumn, Winter have wasted away;
today is the first day of Spring;
and nurse says the sun is shining . . . .
My splints are off;
my limbs feel supple
and I'm running over grass
where the willow lets down her yellow hair.

The door opens and the doctor comes in
returning me to the white cube.
He talks of tests and treatment,
makes no promises.
Improvement is slow.

Visitors come and go
bringing rain on their coats
or a bunch of flowers –
only they bring the weather into my room.
But when they've gone
I'm more alone than before
waiting, watching the door.
The clock ticks on.

PART THREE

UNPUBLISHED POEMS

It's All Been Said Before

I keep my poems small
because all's been said before –
bookshops, libraries, wall to wall
are packed with words,
many unheard as songs of Winter birds.

I keep my poems trim: no space
for ifs and buts, no time
to spin a sentence into rhyme.

I keep my poems close
squeezing the essence into semi-tones,
stripping the flesh to fiddle on the bones.

Not the Poem I Planned

I never write the poem I want to write –
while fingering the net the bird has flown
with coloured fancies out of mind and sight:
no thought is mine to pin down, make my own.

Restless, inhabited, yet still astray,
I pace the vacant rooms, unlock each door
on shadows that surround and melt away
leaving me lost and emptier as before.

I crumple the page, make out a shopping list ......
It gets me as I hurry to the shops;
time moves sideways while my bus is missed;
the world revolves around me, yet it stops.

Not the poem I planned of ancient Greece –
How Hermes' lightning feet were caught in stone,
or Baucis or Philemon turned to trees
while something not of me becomes my own.

Words in Waiting

Beware the word processor
writing your poems for you
with false authority.
Trust the guided hand
that captured the unsought,
unthought out.
Thinking comes later
stoking spontaneous fire
flickering still at mind's edges.

Beware the magpie gleaning
bright beads,
material for stinging
neat as cultured pearls.
Words are there in waiting
for skilled manipulation;
rarely, rarely they rush in
unasked as unexpected
visitors with welcome gifts.

What I Most Dislike

Apart from setting mouse-traps
is writing paper with lines
cramping thought and keeping
ideas confined
to the straight-and-narrow, halting
Imagination with a signed
'on the dotted . . . .' feeling until,
forbidden a writer's coloured moods,
I'm trapped in platitudes.

As for poets whose words are a dance
and a caper,
whoever heard of a poem
laid out cold on ruled paper?

The Cage

I stared at the empty page:
There is my poem, I said.
But the words were birds in a glass cage
And the cage was my head.

Never a sound was uttered;
Not a song to force the lock;
My angry bloodstream uttered;
My heartbeat dead as a clock.

I folded the page, forgot it
But the poem began to grow
Without brain or pen to blot it,
Without time to let me know.

I hoed the garden and weeded,
Thought nothing but soil and grass –
And that was all I needed
To break the glass.

lower case

let us abandon capitals.
letters, like people,
of different shapes and sizes,
associations
must be equal.
the fact that b,d,h,k,l,t
having tops
and g,j,p,q,y
tails
while handwritten f,
father of four-letter words,
flaunts both over sisters and brothers,
reminds us that some
are more equal than others.

The Third Day

*In memory of my son, Richard who died
in a drowning accident.*

'On the third day he rose again.'
Seven words repeated in my head
when the boatmen with the grappling irons
informed us on the third day
that they'd pulled him out.

His innings had been short enough;
at twelve years old he'd not yet courted
the great protector: fear
of roof-tops, frozen ponds and water.
Life was his love
and Perfect love casts out fear.

Our grieving, after all,
was for ourselves; he never knew
such sorrow, never tasted disappointment's dregs,
or felt how anguish stifles joy.

Yet after many years we find,
if not joy, a deep contentment, deep
as the sea,
for many waters cannot quench love.

Loss of Grief

How strangely unfulfilled I am
Since grief has lost its power
To sting and hold me captive
Through every wasted hour.

Intensity is slackened
As feeling drains away:
I can watch the sunset weaken
And the moon rise into day

Till the commonplace absorbs me
In its rhythm; I become
An ordinary person
Whose inner voice is dumb –
I long to be the poet I am
But the words will never come.

The Old Song

In Spring
even sparrow-chirp changes key;
new stations in the air
send leaf-edged signals
of a stir that cannot be pinned
into print, only felt
in prickings under the skin.

There's a lift in the light,
in the swirl
of skirts and heels.
Wheels are caught in the spin
of the sun and colour-tone scales
are sounding an octave higher.

On Putting the Clocks Back

Stop the world for an hour!
Fearing vacancy, boredom, counting
the miles we might cover,
drinks drunk, shots fired, targets hit,
we can't even stop the clocks.

Think
of thousands killed, thousands sown –
so much to do in an hour
and nothing done.

We dare not contemplate the lotus
for fear of seeing ourselves
reflected in the water,
for fear of drowning.

For fear of the future
we put the clocks back.

Arrested

He wears a schoolboy's cap
on his white hair,
rushes into bat
while others of his year
have left the pitch for paths
he could not follow – never saw.

He still laughs
at apple-pie jokes, a mind blunt
as a butter-knife is spared
raw cuts and festering questions
that never penetrate his shell.

Yet even snails have antennae –
this species, differently evolved,
has somewhere hidden from himself
the light of everyman, unless
that first Big Breath has blown it.

Portrait

Framed in all ways –
assessed, marked down, nailed in,
he moved in a measured square
become a nothing, paid performer
of another's will.

Amazingly he grew
tall as a tree, put forth leaves and fruit
to be weighed, measured, bought.
No one measured the root
reaching further than labour and thought.

Came a bad year of shrinking yield.
They removed the frame in which he'd become
less than himself,
left him unsheltered, alone
in a fenceless field.

The long root in silence grown
tugged at his sleeves, drew him on
the longest journey
through railings, bolted doors and walls,
begun the day he was born.

The Wind's Way

The wind has him now
scratching the dust to scatter on the moor
and whirl in the river.
Better this
than a bent twig out of leaf
seeded, spent, he's free.

He's free from the pull of the Spring
that drives us on
without a driver.

The Death of Summer

Watch how the wand of an Autumn morning
Alights
On cold night's silver harvesting.
Bright as a buckle on a dancing sandal
Is dew on these leathery leaves,
On tongues and spurs and laces
And heels of old flowers.
Only the luminous candle
Of Autumn crocus
Sheds a violet illusion
In a corner of Spring,

The thrush's song is thinned;
Marguerites have unpinned
Their Summer stars,
And leaves scrape tinfoil edges in the wind.
A brooch-like bee
Clasps at the heart of a ragged dahlia
Drinks to the death of Summer.

Tidying Up

The big Tidy-Up
is a sort of suicide –
piling the past
with old love letters like old leaves
into a heap for burning:
skeleton memories; outgrown
affinities set alight
in brighter flames than before.
These are real, scorching fingers, feelings
in the impossible. Now ever-moving
out of focus, dimmed
with might-have-beens, diminished
on the present's conveyor-belt,
never pausing for reflection, swept
as paper-boats with paper-lovers
out to sea.

Return to Ribblesdale Place

I've come back – can't you hear
My footsteps on the flagstones, and remember
The way we jumped – or strike me dead –
Over the cracks?
Here is the grid the coalman lifted, shot
Into the dark his noisy bag of coal,
And this is the house where you were born.
Two doors down
The two old ladies with a peacock lived;
Next door up, the strangest pair –
The fat and the thin who went about as one.
Both women and both shunned
By the laced-up ladies of the Place.

Ribblesdale Place; the houses are the same
But where are the people gone?
I knock; nobody comes,
I ring but no one hears
The prodigal daughter waiting on the step
Returned to read the magic number – nine.
My number – nineteen hundred and nine on the twenty-ninth
When I was born to die.

Instead I live in a deaf, deserted world.
Number nine is offices for the Star
Insurance Company – I peer
Through the letter-box; no father, mother, no one
To open letters never posted; no
Young sister hammers on the door.

And what of the garden hidden from the street?
Is the cherry there and the heavy copper beech
Spreading their shade
For clerks and typists in the dinner hour?
If they are felled, the river still must run –
Shining Ribble, running to the sea,
Runs with time and memory away.

The Bridge has gone between us, and the years
Have built the wall.

How can I know you live on the southern side
Beside the river where leaves of cherry and beech
Are never lost?
Am I the shadow
Returning as a ghost?

20th Century Enlightenment

Unwed, pregnant
and never heard of the Pill?
or known the father?
Singularly ill-equipped for giving life –
Let us take it from you.

And travelling by donkey
without a doctor's note?
A case for the psychiatrist –
This
merits abortion.
The state will provide.

An age of enlightenment
cannot abide
fatherless, homeless birth
and afterbirth of hardship, discomfort,
division.
This unseen Light of the World
would show us a way
that few have chosen.

Terminus

Today there are more going in
than coming out.
Tomorrow, when they've learnt the hazards,
may be different.
Today, queues
under the digital clock
flickering seconds like Venetian blinds,
a standing stare
at flashing destinations.
The numbers change in figures of a dance –
arrivals, departures
beating time, advancing
and retreating.

Crowding the barrier
many, dreaming of emigration,
hold paradise passports,
date-palms waving in their heads,
firework birds
exploding into the unknown.

The price of a ticket is return
through an unmapped tunnel.

Academic

When he wakes he'll be searching
bookshops and libraries shelving
away and away in knowledge
receding the faster he reads.
His life is books;
its juices dried on the page –
whole universes counted,
computed, pressed between covers
and bound.

Unthinking she, feet on the grass,
wandering slowly
beside a slow river, has eyes
on the mountain; trees
brush questions to silence;
the wind has no answer . . .
And there he is telling
Voyager's distance from Neptune.

Experts

They unlock doors
we long to open
but, like fairytale children,
are forbidden –
not by any Bluebeard,
but our own ignorance.

Because the scientist
explains the universe,
the psychiatrist
the nature of man,
and the theologian that of God,
we should hold the keys of the Kingdom,
yet are empty-handed.

Experts in analysis
and explanation:
they tell us everything,
weaving facts into patterns;
dance of the planets,
design in cells, and redness of a rose;
caprice of temperament and changing moods,
and –
but here the third falls through the net,
mercifully leaving a space
where God may dwell.

Nameless

There is no use giving a name
to what is written in the wind,
signed on the underside of leaves
and has no form
stamped with date of birth,
present address, nationality
and no identifiable fingerprints.

The archaeologist must accept
the unproven,
and the scientist with test tube and measure
acknowledge the coming of night
without answer.

And what of the theologian
arguing the unanswerable question
that reverberates through centuries
of spire building, bell ringing,
setting up images, performing
rituals, while the killing goes on
and our own comings in and goings out
are certain as the seasons.

York Minster and St. Eadmer's

It's knowing that so many hundreds,
Thousands even, have been here before
To pray or give thanks, or merely for the chance
Of being themselves, that gives the peace
Of anonymity. Loneliness
Is annihilated in becoming part
Of everyone, everything – a mote in the universe.
I am enlarged in such diminishment.

Not the pillars – a beech avenue
Become stone – or the rose window
Filtering the sun through primary colours
That seduce me; it's the silence
Deepened by breath of those
Who breathe no more, whose thoughts
Are woven in the atmosphere.

St. Eadmer's in Bleasdale
Is not like this.
Through the open door
You can smell bracken and heather,
And wind from the moor
Creeps through crevice and keyhole
Like an animal moss-padded,
Insistent, snuffling the dry leaves
Of the open Bible –
Blowing through the organ pipes
The flutes of Pan.

The Only Evergreen

Grey from Saxon sky and stone
is this cold day –
church on its cold hill;
heron alone
on barebone branch, an elegy
for poets long dead.
How words can tread
truth into the heart
as feet tread leaves
in a woodland path,
truth that grieves
for green tongues singing into the wind
of immortality.
Hope is evergreen
that dare not die.

Graveyard on a Hill

Outside Calgary, U.S.A.
is a graveyard set on a hill.
I do not see the tombstones rising grey
and stiff from the soft grass, I see
people standing there, released
in freedom of a dance,
some with arms upraised; others turned
from the east towards the midday sun,
escaped in movement from the captive stone.

Here is rejoicing, meeting, and
reunion such as here we try
to emulate, but cannot quite escape
the coming shadow creeping from behind
which way we look, while they
have stepped beyond our sundown.

Reflections on Mortality

I see people as stones standing,
some upright, some leaning
unmoved by the wind,
all epitaphed by weather,
limned with names and dates.
What is a name
but a sound trailing to echo?
And dates but arbitrary measures
of an episode?

Are they waiting unchanged
or changing as we
hearing other music?
When tides have gone over
refining and grinding,
how shall we hear their voices
grown strange, hollowed as shells
calling beyond our range?

Reflections

I see people in these stones
standing, leaning, never touching
or being touched
except by wind and rain.
Each one's name with dates
spells a lifetime in black letters.

This one says:
I have fought a good fight.
Here in a sheltered corner:
Rest in peace
lacks only a question mark.

Sundown

I love the evening sun
out there, burnishing clouds, fingering
fields and trees
and walls in rooms,
till the dying day blooms again
before it falls;
but not in my eyes
spearing my soul,
seeing through human disguise,
outstaring thought until I'm driven
to sit in shadows that console
and smooth the hot day's hurt.
I'm born again, made whole
in mothering twilight,
waiting for the darkness and the dream
my homesick soul was promised from the start.

Blind Girl's Song

Mine is a world of found and lost,
cold and warm, fur and frost,
of adamant iron, willow that bends
and colours played by my finger-ends.

Mine is a world of timbre and tone;
under the skin I sound the bone;
two worlds in one, beneath the dish
cool and sinuous moves the fish.

Footsteps quiet as snow on grass,
knuckles rapping on wood and glass,
daisies yellow and daisies white,
daybreak, morning, midday, night –
all are one in my world of light.

Reflection

Yes, God,
I'm deeply disturbed by you
whose face buried in cloud
has all Summer avoided
me, your reflection
that cannot shine back into nothing.
Turning towards you
my head drops – a marionette's
whose strings are broken.
Counting the steps that divide us,
I find them shadows
revealing me as a shadow
and you, my substance, concealing
light that would show me myself.

What Is Nothing?

I believe in Nothing.
And what is Nothing?
Space between friend and friend,
star and star.
Space within us
where God is.

Silence of snowfall,
words unspoken,
and footsteps of the dead.

Out of Nothing,
sea, land, animals, trees;
we believe in these.
But what of Nothing,
Invisible, intangible
from which they came?
And which, imprisoned in the senses,
we cannot name.

Credo 1

I believe in Nothing.
And what is Nothing?
Vision behind the eyes,
interval
between heartbeats,
space
between friend and friend,
star and star.

I sit on a bare rock
knowing
I have no purchase, baffled
by silences
between hour and hour
of the clock and season's change
that change millions
of stars and plants and people
into Nothing.

I read what I'm told
to believe; creeds
are nailed to my brain.
But nails rust
as I grow old
and Nothing remains.

The Ballad of Two Stones

Two stones rubbed together
Under a hill;
One starting rolling;
The other lay still.
The one that rolled
Rolled into the town
From Tunstall to Totnes
To Twyford Down,
From London to Leicester
From Yeovil to York
Till it shone like an egg
And started to talk.
The one that lay still
Grew greener each day
Coated in moss with nothing to say.

Winter Song

Why am I sad?
My hands are full of messages;
music of strings
is echoed in voices; even Winter
succumbs to indoor daffodils
while outside remaining flakes
dust the hard edges –
gaps are sharp; hollows never filled
by drifts of snow –
husband, lover, son; depths
unfathomable to look into.

No man can bear nothing;
and he who loves everything
unblinded, knows
that everything comes to nothing in the end.

Poem

Sandgrain, leaf, and drop of rain –
worlds within worlds,
unknowable source, mysterious,
under the microscope
made plain.
Particles, electrons, atoms
counted, assessed, divided
into categories, the unknown
made known.

Out of the original,
wonder is filtered.
Except, of course
in the eyes of a child.

Every Situation Can Be Used to Advantage

Uninvited guests
and overlong stayers
can be used as brick walls
against which to bat your head,
for the exquisite pleasure
in that moment of rising from the sofa
when the room sighs back to itself,
and the transcendent relief
of the final 'good-bye'–
delayed by the half-repeated joke,
the mislaid keys –
like dislodging an obstinate raspberry seed
from between your teeth.

No Score

The price of the holiday,
happy greetings, reunions,
is return
to flowers dead in the dusty vase,
that unopened letter, unread,
the clock stopped.
Silence telling me I am lost,
without identity, without
a life of my own.
I am a player
serving to an empty court,
talking
into the air.
Do you wonder
at those who break off
the game that has no score?

Armchair Travel

Floodlit on its rocky hill
a northern Parthenon,
this Scottish castle edge-to-edge
with grey walls honeyed in the sun
which is Jerusalem.
Next, as the eye moves on,
three gentians' shocking blue against
Iona's sea and sky.
Always sky and sea; always the sun;
flowers perpetually in bloom;
painted villages and native smiles
through grapes and arches;
browning bodies lounging under
red umbrellas *sur la plage*.
For change of scene move no more than your eye.

Poem from My Wheelchair

The cruellest fate of all
is to be aware
of your own deterioration, unable
to walk or carry –
even a tray, yet alert
to the beckoning day
and all that is written or said, aware
of the world passing by
the ground floor window
while you are bound
in a comfortable cell.
And there's always a friend
behind the wheelchair –
you know every crack in the pavement –
and people are kind;
they smile with a shake of the head:
'Your mind is so clear. How lucky you are!'
None can believe I mean what I say
when I say . . . . but it cannot be said.